THE LIEUTENANT OF INISHMORE

BY MARTIN McDONAGH

DRAMATISTS
PLAY SERVICE
INC.

THE LIEUTENANT OF INISHMORE
Copyright © 2003, Martin McDonagh

All Rights Reserved

SPECIAL NOTE

The Lieutenant of Inishmore was first performed
by the Royal Shakespeare Company
at The Other Place, Stratford-upon-Avon, on 11 April 2001.

To Pussy (1981–1995)

THE LIEUTENANT OF INISHMORE was first performed by the Royal Shakespeare Company at The Other Place, Stratford-upon-Avon, England, on April 11, 2001. It was directed by Wilson Milam; the set design was by Francis O'Connor; the lighting design was by Tim Mitchell; the movement was by Jonathan Butterell; the fights were by Terry King; the sound design was by Matt McKenzie; the costume design was by Alastair McArthur; the production manager was Mark Graham; and the stage managers were Hilary Groves (until 9 March) and Martin King (from 9 March). The cast was as follows:

DONNY .... Trevor Cooper
DAVEY .... Owen Sharpe
PADRAIC .... David Wilmot
MAIREAD .... Kerry Condon
JAMES .... Conor Moloney
CHRISTY .... Colin Mace
BRENDAN .... Stuart Goodwin
JOEY .... Glenn Chapman

CHARACTERS

DONNY, mid-forties. Padraic's father. From Inishmore.

DAVEY, seventeen. Slightly overweight, long hair. From Inishmore.

PADRAIC, twenty-one. Handsome. From Inishmore.

MAIREAD, sixteen. Cropped hair, pretty. Davey's sister. From Inishmore.

JAMES, twenties/thirties. Northern Irish.

CHRISTY, thirties/forties. Northern Irish.

BRENDAN, twenty. Northern Irish.

JOEY, twenty. Northern Irish.

PLACE

The island of Inishmore, County Galway.

TIME

The time is 1993.

THE LIEUTENANT OF INISHMORE

SCENE ONE

A cottage on Inishmore circa 1993. Front door in centre of back wall, a window to its left and right. Exit stage left to a bathroom, unseen, an open area forward right to signify another room. A clock somewhere on back wall along with a framed piece of embroidery reading "Home Sweet Home." Cupboards left and right, a telephone on one of them. A couple of armchairs near the back wall and a table centre, on which, as the play begins, lies a dead black cat, its head half missing. Donny, the middle-aged owner of the house, and Davey, a long-haired, slightly pudgy neighbour of seventeen, stand staring quietly at this cat for a few moments.

DAVEY. Do you think he's dead, Donny? *(Pause. Donny picks up the limp dead cat. Bits of its brain plop out. Donny looks across at Davey and puts the cat back down again.)*
DONNY. Aye.
DAVEY. He might be in a coma. Would we ring the vet?
DONNY. It's more than a vet this poor feck needs.
DAVEY. If he gave him an injection?
DONNY. *(Pause.)* Have this injection, you! *(Donny steps back and kicks Davey up the arse.)*
DAVEY. *(Almost crying.)* What was that fer?!
DONNY. How many times have people told you, hairing down that bastarding hill on that bastarding bicycle?

DAVEY. I didn't touch the poor fella, I swear it! In the road I saw him lying…!

DONNY. In the road me arsehole!

DAVEY. And I wasn't hairing at all, I was going slow. And a black lump ahead in the road I saw, and what the devil's that, I said to meself …

DONNY. After you'd rode over him, aye, and then probably reversed!

DAVEY. Ahead in the road, I'm saying, and don't be slinging reversed at me.

DONNY. I'll be slinging what I like!

DAVEY. And I was off me bike be that time anyway and just wheeling it along, and when I saw it was Wee Thomas didn't I scoop him up and run him into you as quick as me legs could carry me?

DONNY. The first thing the books say is don't be moving an accident victim till professional fecking help arrives, and a fool knows that!

DAVEY. Well, I don't be reading books on cats being knocked down, Donny!

DONNY. Well, maybe you should, now …

DAVEY. Because there *are* no such books!

DONNY. … And maybe Thomas would still be with us then.

DAVEY. A car it must have been clobbered him.

DONNY. No cars have been down that road all day, and when do cars ever come down that road? You're the only bastard comes down that lonely road and why? Because you're a cowshite eejit with nothing better to do than roar down roads on your mam's bicycle for no reason other than to feel the wind in that girl's mop o' hair of yours!

DAVEY. If you're insulting me hair again, Donny Osbourne, I'll be off right this minute. After going out of me way to bring your cat in to you …

DONNY. After squashing the life out of me cat, and he isn't my cat at all …

DAVEY. So as not to let the oul flies be picking the meat off him. A favour I was doing you.

DONNY. It's a favour now! With half of that cat's head poking

8

out of the spokes of your wheels, I'll bet, and it's a favour you're doing me! *(Davey stares at Donny a moment, then darts out through the front door. Donny goes over to the cat and strokes it sadly, then sits in the armchair stage left, looking at the cat's blood on his hands. Davey returns a few moments later, dragging his mum's bicycle in through the door. It is pink, with small wheels and a basket. He brings it right over for Donny to see, raises its front wheel so that it's almost in Donny's face, and starts slowly spinning it.)*

DAVEY. Now where's your cat's head? Eh? Now where's your cat's head?

DONNY. *(Depressed.)* Scraping it off on the way wouldn't have been a hard job.

DAVEY. There's no cat's head on that bicycle wheel. Not even a stain, nor the comrade of a stain, and the state of Wee Tommy you'd have had lumps of brain pure dribbling.

DONNY. Put your bicycle out of me face, now, Davey.

DAVEY. Poor Wee Thomas's head, a bicycle wouldn't do damage that decent. Damage that decent you'd have to go out of your way to do.

DONNY. Your bicycle out of me face, I'm saying, or it'll be to your head there'll be decent damage done. *(Davey leaves the bike at the front door.)*

DAVEY. Either a car or a big stone or a dog you'd need to do that decent damage. And you'd hear a dog.

DONNY. And you'd hear a car.

DAVEY. *(Pause.)* You'd probably hear a big stone too. It depends on how big and from what distance. Poor Wee Thomas. I did like him, I did. Which is more than I can say for most of the cats round here. Most of the cats round here I wouldn't give a penny for. They're all full of themselves. Like our Mairead's cat. You'd give him a pat, he'd outright sneer. But Wee Thomas was a friendly cat. He would always say hello to you were you to see him sitting on a wall. *(Pause.)* He won't be saying hello no more, God bless him. Not with that lump of brain gone. *(Pause.)* And you haven't had him long at all, have you, Donny? Wasn't he near brand new?

DONNY. He isn't my fecking cat at all is what the point of the fecking matter is, and you know full well.

DAVEY. I don't know full well. What…?

DONNY. Only fecking looking after the bastard I was the year.

DAVEY. Who were you fecking looking after him for, Donny?

DONNY. Who do you think?

DAVEY. *(Pause.)* Not … not …

DONNY. Not what?

DAVEY. *(With horror.)* Not your … not your …

DONNY. Aye.

DAVEY. No!

DONNY. Why else would I be upset? I don't get upset over cats!

DAVEY. Not your Padraic?!

DONNY. Aye, my Padraic.

DAVEY. Oh Jesus Christ, Donny! Not your Padraic in the INLA?!

DONNY. Do I have another fecking Padraic?

DAVEY. Wee Thomas is his?

DONNY. And was his since he was five years old. His only friend for fifteen year. Brought him out to me when he started moving about the country bombing places and couldn't look after him as decent as he thought needed. His only friend in the world, now.

DAVEY. Was he fond of him?

DONNY. Of course he was fond of him.

DAVEY. Oh he'll be mad.

DONNY. He *will* be mad.

DAVEY. As if he wasn't mad enough already. Padraic's mad enough for seven people. Don't they call him "Mad Padraic"?

DONNY. They do.

DAVEY. Isn't it him the IRA wouldn't let in because he was *too* mad?

DONNY. It was. And he never forgave them for it.

DAVEY. Maybe he's calmed down since he's been travelling.

DONNY. They tell me he's gotten worse. I can just see his face after he hears. And I can just see your face too, after he hears your fault it was. I can see him plugging holes in it with a stick.

DAVEY. *(Dropping to his knees.)* Oh please, Donny, I swear to God it wasn't me. Don't be saying my name to him, now. Sure, Padraic would kill you for sweating near him, let alone this. Didn't he outright cripple the poor fella laughed at that girly scarf he used to wear, and that was when he was twelve?!

DONNY. His first cousin too, that fella was, never minding twelve! And then pinched his wheelchair!

DAVEY. Please now, Donny, you won't be mentioning my name to him? *(Donny gets up and ambles around. Davey stands also.)*

DONNY. If you admit it was you knocked poor Thomas down, Davey, I won't tell him. If you carry on that it wasn't, then I will. Them are your choices.

DAVEY. But it isn't fecking fair, Donny!

DONNY. I don't know if it is or it isn't.

DAVEY. I knew well I should've up and ignored the bastard when I saw him lying there, for if a black cat crossing your path is bad luck, what must one of the feckers lying dead in front of you be? Worse luck. I killed Wee Thomas so, if that's what you want to hear.

DONNY. How?

DAVEY. How? However you fecking want, sure! I hit him with me bike, then I banged him with a hoe, then I jumped up and down on the feck!

DONNY. You hit him with your bike, uh-huh, I suspected. But an accident it was?

DAVEY. An accident, aye. A pure fecking accident.

DONNY. Well … fair enough if an accident is all it was.

DAVEY. *(Pause.)* So you won't be mentioning my name so?

DONNY. I won't be.

DAVEY. Good-oh. *(Pause.)* When'll you be informing him of the news?

DONNY. I'll give him a ring in a minute now. He has a mobile.

DAVEY. He'll be furious.

DONNY. I'll tell him … I'll tell him Wee Thomas is poorly, I'll tell him. Aye …

DAVEY. Sure he'll know he's more than poorly, Donny, when he sees them brains bubbling away …

DONNY. He's poorly but there's no need to be *rushing home,* I'm saying …

DAVEY. I'm with you now, Donny …

DONNY. Do you get me? He's just a tadeen off his food, like, I'll tell him. And in a week I'll say he's going downhill a biteen. And in another week I'll say he passed away peaceful in his sleep, like.

DAVEY. You'll be letting him down easy.

DONNY. I'll be letting him down easy.

DAVEY. You won't give him the bad news all at once. You'll do it in stages, like.

DONNY. The last thing we want is Padraic roaring home to a dead cat, now.

DAVEY. Oh Donny, that's the last thing in the world you'd want.

DONNY. That's the last thing *you'd* want too. You're the bastard brained him, you've admitted. *(Davey goes to say something but doesn't, just squirms.)* Eh?

DAVEY. Aye, aye, I am the bastard ... *(Mumbling.)* for feck's sake ...

DONNY. I'll give him a ring now, I will.

DAVEY. *(Mumbling.)* Give him a ring now, for your fecking self, aye, ya feck. *(Donny stands there biting his bottom lip. Davey goes to the door and picks up his bike.)* Drove on a-fecking-head I should've, I knew! I'm too kind to little things is my fecking trouble! *(Donny picks up the telephone, staring at the cat.)*

DONNY. Oh Wee Tommy, you poor beggar. As fecked up as you are, it mightn't be long till we're just as fecked up as you if that lube turns up. Just as fecked up? Twice as fecked up is more like.

DAVEY. Three times as fecked up probably, Donny, or maybe four times?

DONNY. Be fecking off home you, ya cat brainer.

DAVEY. I will. And I'll be braining some more cats on me way home, cos it's me fecking hobby now, so it is.

DONNY. *(Absently.)* Don't be braining any more cats, now. *(Davey sighs, rolls his eyes to the ceiling and wheels his bike out. Donny starts dialing a number slowly, sadly. Fade to black.)*

SCENE TWO

A desolate Northern Ireland warehouse or some such. James, a bare-chested, bloody and bruised man, hangs upside down from the ceiling, his feet bare and bloody. Padraic idles near him, wielding a cut-throat razor, his hands bloody. Around Padraic's chest are strapped two empty holsters and there are two handguns on a table stage left. James is crying.

PADRAIC. James? *(Pause.)* James?

JAMES. *(Sobbing.)* Wha'?

PADRAIC. Do you know what's next on the agenda?

JAMES. I don't. And I don't want to know.

PADRAIC. I know well you don't, you big feck. Look at the state of you, off bawling like some fool of a girl.

JAMES. Is a fella not supposed to bawl so, you take his fecking toenails off him?

PADRAIC. *(Pause.)* Don't be saying "feck" to me, James ...

JAMES. I'm sorry, Padraic ...

PADRAIC. Or you'll make me want to give you some serious bother, and not just be tinkering with you.

JAMES. Is toenails off just tinkering with me, so?

PADRAIC. It is.

JAMES. Oh, it's just fecking tinkering with me toenails off is ...

PADRAIC. James Hanley, don't keep going on about your stupid fecking toenails! The way you talk it sounds as if I took off a rake of them, when it was only two I took off, and them only small ones. If they'd been big ones I could understand, but they weren't. They were small. You'd hardly notice them gone. And if it was so concerned you were about the health of them toenails it would've been once in a while you cleaned out the muck from under them.

JAMES. Well, you've saved me that job for good now anyways.

PADRAIC. If I hadn't been such a nice fella I would've taken one toenail off of separate feet, but I didn't, I took two toenails off the one foot, so that it's only the one foot you'll have to be limping on and not the two. If it had been the two you'd've found it a devil to be getting about. But with the pain concentrated on the one, if you can get hold of a crutch or a decent stick, I'm not sure if the General Hospital does hand them out but they might do, I don't know. You could phone them up and ask, or go in and see them would be the best thing, and make sure them toes won't be going septic at the same time. I didn't disinfect this razor at all, I never do, I see no need, but they'd be the best people to ask, sure they're the experts. You'll probably need a tetanus jab too, oh there's no question. I do hate injections, I do. I think I'd rather be slashed with a razor than have an injection. I don't know why. Of course, I'd rather have neither. You'll have had both by the end of the day. What a bad day you've had. *(Pause.)* But, em … I have lost me train of thought now, so I have.

JAMES. You've lost your train of thought? Uh-huh. As slow as that fecking train is, and you've lost it?

PADRAIC. *(Pause.)* The next item on the agenda is which nipple of yours do you want to be saying goodbye to. The right or the left?

JAMES. No, now. Come on, now…!

PADRAIC. Be picking, I'm saying! Whichever's your favourite nipple I won't be touching that fella at all, I'll be concentrating on the other. I'll be giving him a nice sliceen and then probably be feeding him to ya, but if you don't pick and pick quick it'll be both of the boys you'll be waving goodbye to, and waving goodbye to two tits when there's no need but to wave goodbye to one makes no sense at all as far as I can see. In *my* eyes, like. In fact it's the mark of a madman. So be picking your nipple and we'll get the ball rolling, for I have better things to do with me time than to be hanging around warehouses cutting *your* nipples off, James Hanley.

JAMES. *(Crying.)* But I've done nothing at all to deserve nipples off, Padraic!

PADRAIC. Oh, let's not be getting into the whys and wherefores, James. You do push your filthy drugs on the schoolchildren of Ireland, and if you concentrated exclusive on the Protestants I'd say all well and good, but you don't, you take all comers.

JAMES. Marijuana to the students at the Tech I sell, and at fair rates…!

PADRAIC. Keeping our youngsters in a drugged-up and idle haze, when it's out on the streets pegging bottles at coppers they should be.

JAMES. Sure, everybody smokes marijuana nowadays.

PADRAIC. I don't!

JAMES. Well, maybe you should! It might calm you down!

PADRAIC. Be picking your nipple, I'm saying!

JAMES. Paul McCartney says it should be outright legalised! He says it's less bad than booze and it cures epileptics!

PADRAIC. Say goodbye to them both so.

JAMES. He has statistics, Padraic! *(Padraic approaches him quickly with the razor.)* The right one! The right one! *(Padraic takes James's right tit in his hand so that the nipple points out, and is just about to slice it off …)*

PADRAIC. Grit your teeth, James. This may hurt.

JAMES. *(Screaming.)* No…! (… *when the cellphone in Padraic's back pocket rings loudly.)*

PADRAIC. Will you hang on there a minute, James…? *(Padraic answers the phone, idling away from James, who is left shaking and whimpering behind him. Into phone.)* Hello? Dad, ya bastard, how are you? *(To James.)* It's me dad. *(Pause.)* I'm grand indeed, Dad, grand. How is all on Inishmore? Good-oh, good-oh. I'm at work at the moment, Dad, was it important now? I'm torturing one of them fellas pushes drugs on wee kids, but I can't say too much over the phone, like …

JAMES. *(Crying.)* *Marijuana,* Padraic.

PADRAIC. They *are* terrible men, and it's like they don't even know they are, when they know well. They think they're doing the world a favour, now. *(Pause.)* I haven't been up to much else, really. I put bombs in a couple of chip shops, but they didn't go off. *(Pause.)* Because chip shops aren't as well guarded as army barracks. Do I need your advice on planting bombs? *(Pause.)* I was pissed off, anyways. The fella who makes our bombs, he's fecking useless. I think he does drink. Either they go off before you're ready or they don't go off at all. One thing about the IRA anyways, as much as I hate the bastards, you've got to hand it to them, they know how to make a decent bomb. *(Pause.)* Sure, why would the IRA be selling us any of their bombs? They need them themselves, sure.

15

Those bastards'd charge the earth anyways. I'll tell ya, I'm getting pissed off with the whole thing. I've been thinking of forming a splinter group. *(Pause.)* I know we're already a splinter group, but there's no law says you can't splinter from a splinter group. A splinter group is the best kind of group to splinter from anyways. It shows you know your own mind, *(Whispering.)* but there's someone in the room, Dad, I can't be talking about splinter groups. *(To James, politely.)* I'll be with you in a minute now, James. *(James shudders slightly.)* What was it you were ringing about anyways, Dad? *(Pause. Padraic's face suddenly becomes very serious, eyes filling with tears.)* Eh? What about Wee Thomas? *(Pause.)* Poorly? How poorly, have you brought him to the doctor? *(Pause.)* *How* long has he been off his food, and why didn't you tell me when it first started? *(Pause.)* He's not too bad? Either he's poorly or he's not too bad now, Dad, he's either one or the fecking other, there's a major difference, now, between not too bad and fecking poorly, he cannot be the fecking two at fecking once, now, *(Crying heavily.)* and you wouldn't be fecking calling me at all if he was not too bad, now! What have you done to Wee Thomas now, you fecking bastard? Put Wee Thomas on the phone. He's sleeping? Well, put a blanket on him and be stroking and stroking him and get a second opinion from the doctor and don't be talking loud near him and I'll be home the first fecking boat in the fecking morning. Ar, you fecker, ya! *(Padraic smashes the phone to pieces on the table, shoots the pieces a few times, then sits there crying quietly. Pause.)*

JAMES. Is anything the matter, Padraic?

PADRAIC. Me cat's poorly, James. Me best friend in the world, he is.

JAMES. What's wrong with him?

PADRAIC. I don't know, now. He's off his food, like.

JAMES. Sure that's nothing to go crying over, being off his food. He probably has ringworm.

PADRAIC. Ringworm? Is that serious, now?

JAMES. Sure, ringworm isn't serious at all. Just get him some ringworm pellets from the chemist and feed them him wrapped up in a bit of cheese. They don't like the taste of ringworm pellets, cats, so if you hide them in a bit of cheese he'll eat them unbeknownst and never know the differ, and he'll be as right as rain in a day or two, or at the outside three. Just don't exceed the stated dose. Y'know, read the instructions, like.

PADRAIC. How do you know so much about ringworm?

JAMES. Sure, don't I have a cat of me own I love with all my heart, had ringworm a month back?

PADRAIC. Do ya? I didn't know drug pushers had cats.

JAMES. Sure, drug pushers are the same as anybody underneath.

PADRAIC. What's his name?

JAMES. Eh?

PADRAIC. What's his name?

JAMES. Em, Dominic. *(Pause.)* And I promise not to sell drugs to children any more, Padraic. On Dominic's life I promise. And that's a big promise, because Dominic means more to me than anything.

PADRAIC. *(Pause.)* Are you gipping me now, James?

JAMES. I'm not gipping you. This is a serious subject. *(Padraic approaches James with the razor and slices through the ropes that bind him. James falls to the floor in a heap, then half picks himself up, testing out his weight on his bloody foot. Padraic holsters his guns.)*

PADRAIC. How are them toes?

JAMES. They're perfect, Padraic.

PADRAIC. You admit you deserved the toes at least?

JAMES. Oh I did. The toes and an arm, really.

PADRAIC. Do you have money to get the bus to the hospital?

JAMES. I don't. *(Padraic gives the confused James some change.)*

PADRAIC. Because you want to get them toes looked at. The last thing you want now is septic toes.

JAMES. Oh d'you know, that's the last thing I'd want.

PADRAIC. I'm off to Galway to see me cat. *(Padraic exits.)*

JAMES. *(Calling out.)* And I hope by the time you get home he's laughing and smiling and as fit as a fiddle, Padraic! *(Pause. Sound of a distant outer door banging shut. Crying.)* I hope that he's dead already and buried in shite, you stupid mental fecking bastard, ya! *(Blackout.)*

SCENE THREE

A country lane. Davey has his bike propped upside down and is lovingly pumping up its tyres. Distinctive whizzing shots from an air rifle begin to sound, one of them hitting Davey in the cheek, making him dive down behind his bike, the others bouncing off the bike itself.

DAVEY. Ar, ya fecker, Mairead! Ya big fecker, you! You got me in the cheek there! *(The shooting stops, Davey whimpering.)*

MAIREAD. *(Off.)* In the cheek, is it?

DAVEY. You could've had me fecking eye out!

MAIREAD. *(Entering.)* That was the object, to have your fecking eye out. I've failed now. *(Mairead is a girl of sixteen or so, slim, pretty, with close-cropped hair, army trousers, white T-shirt, sunglasses. She carries an air rifle and starts kicking Davey's bicycle into the ditch as he gets up, examining his bloody cheek.)*

DAVEY. Leave me fecking bike alone, now! Is it not enough you shoot me in the face, let alone battering me bicycle on top of it?

MAIREAD. No, it's not enough! It's not enough at all for your crimes!

DAVEY. What fecking crimes, ya lube?! Leave me fecking bike, now! *(He shoves Mairead away from the bike. She falls to the ground, then slowly picks herself up, cocks her gun and aims it at Davey's face. Hands raised.)* I didn't mean to push you that hard, Mairead, I promise. *Don't,* now! I'll be telling Mam on ya!

MAIREAD. Go ahead and tell Mam, only you'll have to tell her with no eyes!

DAVEY. What's got into your mad head at all?

MAIREAD. The poor cat you rammed to skitter this morning is what's got into my mad head at all.

DAVEY. Ah, feck, I rammed no cat at all! How did you hear that story?

MAIREAD. The news it was on.

18

DAVEY. It was on no news, and when do you ever watch the news unless there's been a bomb in England gone off you can laugh o'er?

MAIREAD. A little bird did tell me, so.

DAVEY. Well, if he told you I did anything other than ride along slow and see a dead cat in the road and pick it up gentle and run it into Donny's then that little bird is a dirty fecking liar and I'll say it to that bird's fecking face. *(Pause.)* That was the entire of it, Mairead. Sure, I have as much concern for the cats of this world as you do, only I don't go around saying it, because if I went around saying it they'd call me an outright gayboy, and they do enough of that with me hairstyle. *(Mairead lowers the gun and idles around.)* You'd have blinded your brother over a dead cat.

MAIREAD. I would. Without a question.

DAVEY. And then you say you're not mad.

MAIREAD. I'm not at all mad.

DAVEY. I could round up ten cows with only one eye would disagree.

MAIREAD. Don't keep bringing them cows' eyes up! Them cows' eyes was a political protest!

DAVEY. Against cows? Sure, what have cows done?

MAIREAD. Against the fecking meat trade, and you know well!

DAVEY. I can't see how shooting cows in the eyes is going to do any damage to the meat trade, now.

MAIREAD. Of course you can't, because you're a thick. Don't you know that if you take the profit out of the meat trade it'll collapse in on itself entirely, and there's no profit at all in taking ten blind cows to market, I'll tell ya. There's a loss. For who would want to buy a blind cow?

DAVEY. No one.

MAIREAD. No one is right. So in those circumstances I did see cows as valid targets, though my thinking has gone full tilt since then, and they are valid targets no longer.

DAVEY. Aye. It's only wee lads and their bicycles you see as valid targets nowadays.

MAIREAD. If they're suspected of doing damage to cats it is, aye.

DAVEY. Well, I was doing no damage to that cat. I was trying to help that cat, and help Donny too, and amn't I still trying to help Donny, running arse-faced errands I'm a dead man if I fail in.

MAIREAD. What errands?

DAVEY. He's got me roaming the country to find a black cat identical to his Wee Thomas, so that when Padraic roars home at high noon tomorrow it won't be a cat with a half a head we'll be placing in his arms.

MAIREAD. Sure, do you think Padraic's thick?

DAVEY. What we're banking on is that Padraic's as thick as a mongo fecking halfwit. *(Mairead pokes his bloody cheek.)*

MAIREAD. Don't be saying mongo halfwit about a brave son of Erin, now, David!

DAVEY. I won't be, Mairead.

MAIREAD. Padraic'll be able to tell the differ straight off between a cat that's his and a cat that isn't. Sure, isn't he a second-lieutenant at the age of twenty-one, sure?

DAVEY. He is, aye, a second-lieutenant. In his own brain if nowhere else.

MAIREAD. Sure, every cat has its own separate personality, sure, not to mention its eyes and its miaow. Look at my Sir Roger. Sir Roger has a different personality to any cat. Any cat I've ever known, anyways ...

DAVEY. Aye. He's a snooty little bitch.

MAIREAD. He's no snooty little bitch.

DAVEY. He's a snooty bitch and he tore two of me *X-men* comics the other day and on purpose ...

MAIREAD. Good on Sir Roger, so.

DAVEY. So don't be defending him.

MAIREAD. I will do what I wish.

DAVEY. Is me cheek still bleeding?

MAIREAD. It is.

DAVEY. *(Quietly.)* Ya feck. *(Davey sets up his bike again and starts pumping it as before. Mairead idles, swinging her gun around her fingers and singing "The Dying Rebel.")*

MAIREAD. *(Singing.)* "The last I met was a dying rebel ... "

DAVEY. Ar, don't be singing your fool fecking rebel songs again, now, Mairead!

MAIREAD. *(Singing.)* "Kneeling low I heard him say, God bless my home in dear Cork City, God bless the cause for which I die."

DAVEY. *(Singing over her last line — Motorhead.)* "The ace of spades! The ace of spades!" *(Christy, Northern Irish, in a dark suit, sporting an eye-patch, enters right, walking along the road. He stops as he's about to pass the two.)*

CHRISTY. Howdo?

DAVEY. Howdo?

CHRISTY. That's a nice wee gun.

MAIREAD. It gets the job done.

CHRISTY. *(To Davey.)* I've seen you somewhere before, I'm thinking.

DAVEY. I don't know if you have or you haven't.

CHRISTY. Today, even, it may've been. I remember your girly hair. *(Davey tuts.)* Weren't you the fella I saw rode over the cat on the road this morning?

DAVEY. I rid over no cat! *(Mairead backs off, stern-faced, sits on a rock stage left and stares at Davey throughout. Davey is aware of this, nervous.)*

CHRISTY. Did you not, now? I must be mistaken, so.

DAVEY. I rode *up to* a cat, slow, and when I saw he was in a bad way I ran him into the fella he belongs to to try and save him, as fast as me legs could carry me.

CHRISTY. The fella whose he is must've been upset.

DAVEY. He *was* upset. And the cat isn't even his either. It's another fella's.

CHRISTY. Is that fella upset?

DAVEY. He will be tomorrow when he gets home. He thinks it's only poorly. It isn't poorly. It's buried in his potatoes.

CHRISTY. Uh-huh. What time will this other fella be home?

DAVEY. Uh … twelve, I think. Aye, twelve. *(Christy nods and begins to walk off stage left.)*

CHRISTY. All the best to yous.

DAVEY. Fella? Will you tell me sister you were wrong when you said I rid over that cat? Isn't it right you only saw me ride up to it, slow, like, if anything at all you saw?

CHRISTY. *(Pause.)* I was brought up be Jesuits. And the thing the Jesuits tell you, "It's a terrible thing to go lying." Of course, a fella's eyes can often play tricks on him, especially when he only has one eye, but as sure as shite I'd swear you aimed for that cat's head full-pelt, then near enough reversed on the fecker. I'll be seeing you. (*Christy exits stage left. Mairead cocks her rifle.*)

DAVEY. I did no such … (*Davey sprints off stage right, covering his face as he goes. Mairead shoots after him, then kicks his bicycle over and starts shooting at it. Slow fade to black.*)

MAIREAD. And only the fecking start this is, Davey Claven! You'll be dead as that cat be the time this is over, if not more dead, ya feck, ya!

SCENE FOUR

Night. Donny's house. Donny is standing, swigging poteen from the bottle, his hands black, watching Davey trying to cover a ginger cat in black shoe polish and doing a very poor job of it. Both men are very drunk.

DONNY. He'll suspect.

DAVEY. He won't.

DONNY. (*Pause.*) He will, now.

DAVEY. I amn't half finished yet. Don't be criticising until you've seen the finished job now, Donny. (*Donny staggers to the armchair left and sits, taking another swig.*) And don't be hogging that poteen.

DONNY. It is my poteen to hog. (*Davey goes over and takes a swig himself, then continues on the cat.*) As soon as he walks through the door he'll know that isn't his cat. Sure that cat's orange.

DAVEY. He won't be orange by the time I've finished with the feck. He'll be black as a coon.

DONNY. You should've got a black cat at the outset, never minding coons. (*Davey waves the cat in the air.*)

DAVEY. If you don't like the cat I got you then I'll take the fecker and go. We didn't come here to be criticised.

DONNY. Stay and be finishing, ya long-haired goob. Be putting some on his gob, there. He's pure orange on his gob.

DAVEY. (*Continuing painting the cat.*) Five mile I roamed looking for a black cat, and walking, after me bitch sister bashed up me bicycle, and no black cats was there, or if there was they was being played with be children, and I am no man to be pinching cats off of children.

DONNY. Aye. No guts for the job. I knew well.

DAVEY. It isn't guts at all. It's having enough of a heart not to make poor gasurs go crying. *(Mumbled.)* And their mams were there anyways.

DONNY. I'll bet their mams were there. And if you were any kind of a man at all you'd've walked up to them mams and said "I'm taking yere kids' cat," and if they'd put up a show you could've given them a belt, and then trampled on the bitches!

DAVEY. I'm no man to go trampling on mams. Not for the sake of a cat anyways. Would you've liked your mam trampled on when she was alive?

DONNY. Many's the time I trampled on my mam when she was alive. After she'd died I stopped. There seemed no sense.

DAVEY. What did you go trampling on your mam for?

DONNY. Ah, she'd get on me nerves.

DAVEY. I can see where your Padraic does get his outlook on life now.

DONNY. That awful, hairy chin on her. *(Pause.)* Let me have a crack at that cat, now. You do a poor job of cat covering. *(Donny gets up and Davey lets him take over, sitting down with the poteen.)*

DAVEY. I was trying to make the polish go further. There's hardly a smatter left.

DONNY. If you knew it was an orange cat you were bringing you should've brought your own shoe polish, and not go skittering away mine.

DAVEY. Is it orders you're pegging me now?

DONNY. You should've come prepared. This cat's going to end up only half black, and if he goes licking himself in the night on top of it, the jig'll truly be up, boy.

DAVEY. *(Pause.)* Cats are forever licking themselves. I don't know why. More than dogs. It must be something in their brains. Aye.

DONNY. *(Funny voice.)* I am putting some on your head now, baby, be closing your eyes so they will not be stinging and you would go crying.

DAVEY. That cat's an awful cry-baby.

DONNY. Where did you get this cat?

DAVEY. Ah, just off somebody.

DONNY. It does have a tag. What's its name, now…?

DAVEY. Sir Roger.

DONNY. Sir Roger. That's a funny name for a cat.

DAVEY. It is. It was probably some mental case named that cat.

DONNY. Will I take his name tag off, Davey? Else that'd give the game away straight off.

DAVEY. Take it off, aye, else Padraic'd be reading it and know straight off by the name it wasn't Wee Thomas. That was intelligent thinking, Donny.

DONNY. I know well it was. I don't need your opinion on my intelligencientiousness. (*Donny tosses the name tag on to a cupboard left.*)

DAVEY. (*Pause.*) We could tell him Wee Thomas has a disease makes him go orangey-looking.

DONNY. We could, d'you know?

DAVEY. And smell of shoe polish.

DONNY. Do you think that'd work, Davey?

DAVEY. No.

DONNY. What did you fecking say it for, so?

DAVEY. Just for the sake of it, Donny. (*Donny tuts.*) Was that true, Donny, about you trampling on your mam, now?

DONNY. (*Smiling.*) I was exaggerating a biteen.

DAVEY. I was thinking.

DONNY. I did kick her once but that was all I did.

DAVEY. I was thinking. Your mam'd have to have done something awful wrong for you to go trampling on her. I love my mam. Love her more than anything. Love her more than anything. (*Donny is almost running out of shoe polish. The cat is less than half covered, looking completely ridiculous.*) Mm. I do like the smell of shoe polish, I do.

DONNY. The same as that, I do. (*The two of them sniff their black hands deeply.*) It does make you want to eat it.

DAVEY. It does. Have you ever tried it?

DONNY. When I was young.

DAVEY. The same as that. Isn't it coarse?

DONNY. It is. And they know what you've been doing be the

state of your tongue.

DAVEY. And then they laugh at you.

DONNY. Aye. *(Pause.)* There we go, now ... *(He finishes polishing the cat, then holds him up high in the air for Davey to see.)* What do you think, Davey? Will we get away with it? *(Davey considers for a few moments.)*

DAVEY. He'll put a gun to our heads and blow out what little brains we have.

DONNY. *(Laughing.)* He will! *(Blackout.)*

SCENE FIVE

Roadside. Night. Christy, Brendan and Joey, who sits apart from the other two. Christy eats beans from a can. All have Northern Irish accents.

CHRISTY. Come over and eat some beans, you.

JOEY. I don't eat beans with fellas the likes of ye.

BRENDAN. The babby's going crying now.

JOEY. I'm not going crying either.

CHRISTY. Don't start arguing again, you two.

BRENDAN. Shitting his knickers at the job he has in hand.

JOEY. Shitting me knickers? Do you want to see me knickers to see if they're shitted?

BRENDAN. I don't!

JOEY. No shit is there at all in my knickers. I've the balls to take on any feck. No matter how big or grand. But what I don't have, I don't have to go out of me way to pick on wee fellas I'm twenty times bigger than and who are unarmed, and who never will be armed because they have no arms. Just paws.

CHRISTY. We none of us enjoyed today's business, Joey-o, but hasn't the plan worked? And like the fella said, "Don't the ends justify the means?" Wasn't it Marx said that, now? I think it was.

BRENDAN. It wasn't Marx, no.

CHRISTY. Who was it then?

BRENDAN. I don't know, now. It wasn't Marx is all I'm saying.

CHRISTY. Oh, Brendan, you're always cutting people down and saying who didn't say things. A fool can say who didn't say things. It takes intelligence to put your neck on the line and say who did say things.

BRENDAN. I suppose it does, but it wasn't Marx, is all I'm saying.

CHRISTY. So who was it then?

BRENDAN. I don't know!

CHRISTY. It was some feck to do with Russia!

BRENDAN. It may have been, and it probably was. It sounds like something them fecks would say. What I'm saying, Christy, it wasn't fecking Marx, now!

CHRISTY. There's no talking to this fella.

BRENDAN. Not on the subject of quotes, no.

JOEY. *(Pause.)* Ye've changed the subject on me.

CHRISTY. What was the subject?

JOEY. Battering in the head of an innocent cat was the subject! I don't remember agreeing to batter cats when I joined the INLA.

BRENDAN. What cat did you batter? Me and Christy battered that cat without a lick o' help from you.

JOEY. Being *associated* with cat battering, I'm saying.

BRENDAN. Well, don't claim credit for battering a cat you never lifted a finger to batter.

JOEY. I won't claim credit for battering a cat, because there *is* no credit in battering a cat. Battering a cat is easy. There's no guts involved in cat battering. That sounds like something the fecking British'd do. Round up some poor Irish cats and give them a blast in the back as the poor devils were trying to get away, like on Bloody Sunday.

BRENDAN. They never shot cats on Bloody Sunday, did they, Christy?

JOEY. It's the same principle I'm saying, ya thick.

BRENDAN. Oh, the same principle.

JOEY. I'd've never joined the INLA in the first place if I'd known the battering of cats was to be on the agenda. The INLA has gone down in my estimation today. Same as when we blew up Airey Neave. You can't blow up a fella just because he has a funny name.

It wasn't his fault.

CHRISTY. Why don't you form a splinter group, so, like oul Mad Padraic?

BRENDAN. Aye. The Irish National Being Nice To Cats Army.

JOEY. I would. Only I know you two'd blow me away for it, after probably killing me goldfish first!

BRENDAN. Sure, you've no goldfish, Joey.

JOEY. I was making a fecking comparison!

CHRISTY. *(Pause.)* We none of us enjoyed killing that cat, Joey-o. I was near crying meself, even as I brought me gun swinging down the fourth and fifth times, and the blood spraying out of him. But hasn't it worked? Haven't we lured the Madman of Aran home to where never once will he be looking behind him for that bolt from the blue he knows is some day coming? It won't be so quick then he'll be to go forming splinter groups, and knocking down fellas like poor Skank Toby, fellas who only do the community a service, and do they force anybody to buy their drugs? No. And don't they pay us a pound on every bag they push to go freeing Ireland for them? Isn't it for everybody we're out freeing Ireland? That's what Padraic doesn't understand, is it isn't only for the school kids and the oul fellas and the babes unborn we're out freeing Ireland. No. It's for the junkies, the thieves and the drug pushers too!

JOEY. Aye. And for the cat batterers on top of it! *(Brendan and Christy stare hatefully at Joey a second, then slowly get up, spread out, take out their guns and point them at him. Joey, scared, stands and points his gun back at them.)*

CHRISTY. I was making a good speech there and you ruined it!

BRENDAN. He did, Christy. He ruined your speech on you. Let's pepper him.

JOEY. Ah, let's not point our guns at each other. Sure, we're all friends here.

CHRISTY. I thought we were friends, aye, but then you keep dragging dead cats into the equation.

JOEY. I'm sorry, Christy. I have a fondness for cats is all. I'm sorry.

CHRISTY. You want to get your priorities right, boy. Is it happy cats or is it an Ireland free we're after?

JOEY. It's an Ireland free, Christy. Although I'd like a combination of the two. *(Christy cocks his gun.)* It's an Ireland free, Christy.

(Pause. Christy lowers his gun and collects his belongings. After a second the other two put their guns away also.)

CHRISTY. Good. For won't the cats of Ireland be happier too when they won't have the English coming over bothering them no more?

JOEY. They will.

CHRISTY. Do you know how many cats Oliver Cromwell killed in his time?

BRENDAN. Lots of cats.

CHRISTY. Lots of cats. And burned them alive. We have a way to go before we're in that bastard's league. We'll have not another word on the cat matter. Collect up your gear. We'll lie low in a barn or somewhere tonight. Twelve noon the little fat lad said Padraic wouldn't be home till, and he had no need to lie. We'll arrive at ten past, and enter blasting. *(The others collect their gear and move off left.)* Did I tell you how I fecked up the fat fecker with his sister, saying it was him killed the cat? I said, "The Jesuits say you should never tell a lie, boy, so I'll have to tell the truth on that subject." Ha ha.

BRENDAN. Except it isn't the Jesuits who say that at all.

CHRISTY. Is it not? Who is it then?

BRENDAN. I don't know, but it isn't the Jesuits.

CHRISTY. Are you starting again?

BRENDAN. Starting what?

CHRISTY. Starting your saying who didn't say things.

BRENDAN. I'm not starting anything. I'm just saying it isn't the Jesuits.

CHRISTY. So who is it?

BRENDAN. I don't know!

CHRISTY. I suppose it was fecking Marx!

BRENDAN. *(Exiting.)* It may have been fecking Marx. I do not know. What I'm saying for sure is it isn't the fecking Jesuits.

CHRISTY. *(Exiting.)* Get ahead on the fecking road, you! *(The voices of the three fade to mumbles offstage. Pause. Mairead idles on from stage right, having overheard their conversation. She stares off after the men a second, broods thoughtfully, then cocks her air rifle. Blackout.)*

SCENE SIX

Another roadside. Night, moonlight. Mairead, in lipstick and a little make-up for once, leans against a wall, singing quietly "The Patriot Game," the air rifle on the wall beside her.

MAIREAD. *(Singing.)* "Come all ye young rebels and list while I sing. The love of one's land is a terrible thing. It banishes fear with the speed of a flame, and it makes us all part of the patriot game." *(Padraic enters right and slowly moves along the road towards her. Though she's noticed him she continues singing. Singing.)* "Oh my name is O'Hanlon, and I've just gone sixteen. My home is in Monaghan, there I was weaned. I was taught all my life cruel England's to blame, and so I'm a part of the patriot game." *(Padraic stops in front of her, having joined in on her last line. They look at each other a while.)*
PADRAIC. It's a while since I heard that oul song. Wasn't it one of the Behans wrote that?
MAIREAD. It was. Dominic.
PADRAIC. *(About to move on.)* If they'd done a little more bombing and a little less writing I'd've had more respect for them.
MAIREAD. I still have respect for them. Lieutenant.
PADRAIC. *(Pause.)* You're not Seamus Claven's daughter?
MAIREAD. I am. You remembered me, so.
PADRAIC. I remember you chasing me begging to bring you when I left to free the North, and that when you were ten.
MAIREAD. Eleven. I'm sixteen now. If you get me meaning. Haven't I grown up since?
PADRAIC. You have. Upwards if not outwards. From a distance I thought "What's a boy doing sitting there with lipstick on?," then as I got closer I realised it was a lass, just with shocking hair.
MAIREAD. *(Hiding hurt.)* Is that a nice thing to say to a girl comes to meet you off the boat the early morning?
PADRAIC. I suppose it's not, but that's the way I am.
MAIREAD. The girls must be falling over themselves to get to you

29

in Ulster so, if them's the kind of compliments you be paying them.

PADRAIC. A few have fallen but I paid no mind. Not while there was work to be done ridding Erin of them jackboot hirelings of England's foul monarchy, and a lot of the girls up North are dogs anyways, so it was no loss.

MAIREAD. Do you prefer Inishmore girls, so?

PADRAIC. I don't.

MAIREAD. You don't prefer boys?

PADRAIC. I do not prefer boys! There's no boy-preferers involved in Irish terrorism, I'll tell you that! They stipulate when you join.

MAIREAD. Good, cos there's a dance at the church hall Friday would you take me to?

PADRAIC. Amn't I after telling you? I'm interested in no social activities that don't involve the freeing of Ulster.

MAIREAD. But that narrows it down terrible.

PADRAIC. So be it.

MAIREAD. *(Pause.)* There's a film on at the Omniplex about the Guildford Four next week. Isn't that close enough?

PADRAIC. Ah, feck the Guildford Four. Even if they didn't do it, they should've took the blame and been proud. But no, they did nothing but whine.

MAIREAD. We could go Dutch!

PADRAIC. *(Gently.)* No, Mairead. *(Pause.)* Why *did* you come to meet me this far out of your way?

MAIREAD. *(Sulkily.)* No reason.

PADRAIC. Just to ask me out, was it? Ah. *(Ruffles her hair.)* I see you still have your oul popgun there you wanted to give me that day. A lot of use that would've been to me up North.

MAIREAD. It does do the job for me OK.

PADRAIC. I suppose it does. There's not a heifer left with eyesight on Aran, I'll bet.

MAIREAD. *(Pacing angrily.)* Everybody slings me cow blinding at me, no matter how many years go by! What nobody ever mentions is it was from sixty yards I hit them cows' eyes, which is bloody good shooting in anybody's books. If I'd walked bang up to them I could understand it, but I didn't, I gave them every chance.

PADRAIC. Ah, hold your horses, Mairead, I was only fooling with you. I meself once shot a fella in the eye with a crossbow, but that was from right next to him. Sixty yards is marvellous going.

MAIREAD. You can't be getting round me that easy …

PADRAIC. Mairead, now …

MAIREAD. And you can forget the message I had for you too!

PADRAIC. What message?

MAIREAD. No message.

PADRAIC. No, what message did you have for me? *(Suddenly upset, suspicious.)* It wasn't me cat the message was about?

MAIREAD. If it was or if it wasn't I don't know, I have forgot. *(Padraic angrily pulls out both his guns and points them at Mairead's head.)*

PADRAIC. Tell me the fecking message now, ya bitcheen! Has me cat gone downhill or what the feck is it? Eh? *(Poised, disgusted and superior, Mairead picks up her air rifle, cocks it, and, while Padraic still has his guns to her head, points the rifle towards one of his eyes, so that the barrel is almost resting against it. Pause.)* Do you think I'm joking?

MAIREAD. Do you think I am?

PADRAIC. *(Long pause.)* You have some balls, anyways.

MAIREAD. I don't have.

PADRAIC. I'll take your word. *(Padraic lowers his guns. Mairead pauses a moment or two, her rifle still up to his face, then she lowers it also.)*

MAIREAD. Will you let me join up this time when you go back, so, if I'm such a tough oul feck with balls?

PADRAIC. We don't be letting girls in the INLA. No. Unless pretty girls. What was the message?

MAIREAD. *(Almost tearful.)* Unless pretty girls? Not even middling-looking girls who can put a cow's eye out from sixty yards?

PADRAIC. No. We have no call for girls with them attributes.

MAIREAD. Unfair to women that sounds.

PADRAIC. No, just fair to cows. *(Pause.)* What was the message, Mairead? Was it about my Wee Thomas, now?

MAIREAD. Your final word on the matter is you won't let me in the INLA, so? Not ever?

PADRAIC. Not as long as I have any say in the INLA. It's for your own good I'm saying this, Mairead. Be staying home, now, and marry some nice fella. Let your hair grow out a tadeen and some fella's bound to be looking twice at you some day, and if you learn how to cook and sew too, sure, that'd double your chances. Maybe treble.

MAIREAD. *(Pause.)* The message was Wee Thomas is over the worst of it, but be hurrying home to him, just to be on the safe side, now.

PADRAIC. He's over the worst of it?

MAIREAD. He is.

PADRAIC. *(Ecstatic.)* Oh, God love you, Mairead, I could kiss you! *(Padraic grabs Mairead in his arms and kisses her, a kiss of thanks at first, which lengthens into something much more sensual. They break, both a little disturbed. Padraic smiles uncomfortably and hurries off stage left. Mairead stares at the ground a while, singing quietly to herself, but with a little more thought for the words than before.)*

MAIREAD. *(Singing.)* "And now as I lie with my body all holed ... I think of the traitors who bargained and sold ... And I'm sorry my rifle has not done the same ... for the Quislings who sold out the patriot game." *(Mairead looks off stage left after Padraic. Blackout.)*

SCENE SEVEN

Early blue dawn. Donny's house. Five o'clock. Donny and Davey still boozed, Donny in the armchair left, sleepy, Davey sitting on the floor right, holding a wooden cross he's made, its lower piece sharpened to a point, and along the crosspiece of which he finger-paints in shoe polish the words "Wee Thomas." The shoe-polished cat from earlier idles around where he pleases. Empty cat basket on table left.

DONNY. Remember now.

DAVEY. I'll remember. *(Pause.)* Remember what?

DONNY. To be waking me!

DAVEY. Aye.

DONNY. There's nothing more can be done till we're sober and it's light out, so we'll have a wee sleep and be up bright and early to fix the final touches so not a thing will he suspect.

DAVEY. Aye.

DONNY. So be remembering to be waking me.

DAVEY. *(Yawning.)* I will.

DONNY. You're a light sleeper, so you say.

DAVEY. I'm an awful light sleeper. Not only that, I have a thing in me head I can force meself to wake up bang on any hour I've decided on the night before. And not only the hour. The minute! Y'know, like a ninja.

DONNY. How did you get that in your head?

DAVEY. It's a thing I've had since I was a child.

DONNY. Creepy, that sounds.

DAVEY. Aye, it is creepy.

DONNY. Set your head for nine in the morning, so.

DAVEY. Me head is set, you do not have to ask.

DONNY. *(Pause.)* What's that you're doing? *(Davey shows Donny the finished cross.)*

DAVEY. It's a cross for Wee Thomas. Look, it says "Wee Thomas."

DONNY. That's a well-made cross.

DAVEY. *I* think it is, but it has to be drying, now. *(Davey sets the cross face down on the floor, taps it for luck, puts the cat in the cat basket, giving him a pat, and goes and sits in the armchair right, huddling up in it for sleep.)*

DONNY. In the morning, too, we'll have to go over the place with a toothcomb to make sure we've left nothing to give the game away his cat's dead.

DAVEY. We will, aye, although I think we've covered everything.

DONNY. *(Pause.)* And you'll be remembering to wake me?

DAVEY. Me head is set for nine, Donny. I'm going to get angry soon.

DONNY. Nighty-night, so.

DAVEY. Nighty-night, aye.

DONNY. Don't let the bedbugs be biting.

DAVEY. I won't let them. *(The two men sit there, falling asleep. Slow fade to black.)*

DONNY. And you'll remember to be waking me? *(Davey looks across at Donny sternly. Donny sniggers. Davey laughs too. They settle down to sleep.)*

SCENE EIGHT

Donny's house. Twelve noon. Donny and Davey asleep in their armchairs, hands still black. Thomas' cross still lying on the floor, the polished cat asleep in the cat basket, only half visible, purring. Padraic enters through the front door quietly, happily and, on seeing the two men asleep, calls out in a whisper, looking for his cat.

PADRAIC. Thomas? Wee Thomas? Here, baby. Daddy's home. Are you not well, loveen? I've some ringworm pellets here for ya. *(Pause. Padraic notices the cat asleep in the basket, goes over to it and, confused, runs his fingers along its back. His fingers come away black and he smells them. He idles back to the sleeping Davey, spots Davey's black hands, raises one of them to get a better look at it, then lets it drop. Davey remains asleep. Still confused, Padraic notices the cross on the floor and picks it up. As he reads its inscription his face drops, from sadness to fury, just as Davey begins to wake, stretch his arms, open his eyes and see Padraic.)*
DAVEY. Feck me! *(Padraic storms over to Davey, wrenches him up by the hair, takes a gun out and points it at Davey's head. Davey whimpers, waking Donny.)*
PADRAIC. *(To Davey.)* Where's me cat? Eh? Where's me fecking cat?
DONNY. *(Sleepily.)* Are you home, Padraic?
DAVEY. I forgot to wake you, Donny!
PADRAIC. Where's me fecking cat, I said? *(Still whimpering, Davey points a shaky finger at the cat basket. Donny, regaining his senses, is now fearful too.)*
PADRAIC. Eh?
DONNY. He has a disease makes him go orangey, Padraic.
PADRAIC. Oh, he has a disease makes him go orangey, does he?
DAVEY. *(High-pitched, breathless.)* And smell of shoe polish! *(Padraic drags Davey to the cat basket. Donny stands.)*

34

PADRAIC. So this is Wee Thomas, is it?

DONNY. It is.

DAVEY. It is.

DONNY. We think.

PADRAIC. Oh, hello there, Wee Thomas. It's nice to be seeing you again after all this time.

DONNY. I suppose he's changed since last you saw him, Padraic. Oh, cats do change quick.

PADRAIC. Changed quick, is it, Dad? *(He shoots the sleeping cat, point blank. It explodes in a ball of blood and bones. Davey begins screaming hysterically. Donny puts his hands to his head. Padraic shoves Davey's face into the bloody cat to stop him screaming.)* He's changed quick enough now! And ye two'll be changing the same way in a minute. Where's Wee Thomas? For the fiftieth fecking time, this is!

DONNY. We think he's run away!

PADRAIC. You think he's run away, do ye? *(He takes Davey's head out of the cat, forces him to his knees, lunges over to Donny, grabs him by the hair and kneels him down beside Davey.)* Is that why these shenanigans? *(Padraic angrily holds up the dead bloody cat from the basket, then throws it in through the door to the bathroom stage left.)* Is that why this fecking thing, so? *(Padraic bangs Donny in the face with the crucifix and holds it in front of him.)*

DONNY. *(To Davey.)* I knew you'd made a mistake somewhere along the line, you!

PADRAIC. Is Wee Thomas dead, now? Answer me!

DONNY. *(Pause.)* He is, Padraic. *(Padraic puts his head in his hands and lets out a long, deep moan, backing off around the room.)*

DAVEY. We did see him in the road, Padraic …

DONNY. We didn't see him in the road at all, Padraic. This fella clobbered him with his bike and then pegged stones at him.

DAVEY. Not at all, Padraic!

DONNY. Admitted, he has!

DAVEY. Ahead in the lonely road I saw him lying, and ran him inside then as quick as me legs could carry me, and me only crime, if I have one at all, was moving the victim before professional help arrived, but with Wee Tommy's head strung a mile o'er the road, I assumed the niceties wouldn't be necessry.

35

DONNY. And pegged stones, Padraic.

DAVEY. Pegged stones me arse! This from a fella feeds his cat nothing but Frosties.

DONNY. I do not feed him Frosties, Padraic! I buy cat food and *good* cat food. Sheba half the time, I buy.

DAVEY. Sheba bollocks, and I'll give you a pound if any Sheba you can find in this feck's cupboards …

PADRAIC. *(Screaming.)* Shut up!!

DONNY. I *do* buy Sheba, Padraic … *(Padraic rifles through a couple of drawers until he finds some rope, which he then uses to tie Donny's hands to his feet behind his back. Donny, scared:)* Oh, Padraic, don't be tying me hands behind me back, now. We know what you be doing to fellas their hands you tie behind their back …

DAVEY. What does he be doing to them, Donny? Tickling them. *(Donny gives him a look. Davey, crying:)* I was just trying to keep me hopes up. *(Padraic ties Davey in the same way as Donny, during which Davey manages to get up some nerve. Angrily:)* Sure, I was only trying to save the feck was how I became involved!

PADRAIC. So me cat is a feck now, is he?

DAVEY. He is! And you are too, Padraic Osbourne! And I don't care if you do blow the head off me. You're a mad thick feck and everybody knows that you are! So there!

DONNY. *(Shocked.)* Oh, Davey boy …

PADRAIC. Let's see you with a bit of a haircut, so, if I'm such a mad thick feck. *(Padraic takes out a bowie knife and starts roughly hacking off all of Davey's hair.)*

DAVEY. Ar, not me hair! Sure, this just confirms you're a mad thick feck!

PADRAIC. I'd be scared the bullets wouldn't be getting through this girl's minge.

DONNY. Ah, don't be killing us, Padraic. Sure, we didn't mean for Wee Thomas to die.

PADRAIC. Wee Thomas was in your care. Me only friend in the world for fifteen years, and then into your care I put him …

DAVEY. Fifteen years? Sure, he'd had a good innings, Padraic. Aargh!

PADRAIC. And Wee Thomas is now dead. Them's the only facts this tribunal needs.

DONNY. What tribunal?

DAVEY. Them facts are only circumstantial. *(The haircut finished, Padraic tosses the knife aside and takes out his two handguns.)*

PADRAIC. These guns are only circumstantial, so, and so too your brains'll be only circumstantial as they leave your heads and go skidding up the wall.

DAVEY. That sentence makes no sense at all.

DONNY. *(To Davey.)* Do you have to get him even more worked up, you? *(Padraic puts a gun to the back of each of their heads.)*

PADRAIC. Be making any final confession you have, now, before you go meeting yere maker. Maybe a rabbit you knifed, or a pony you throttled.

DAVEY. I'm making no confession because there's nothing in the world I've done wrong.

PADRAIC. *(To Donny.)* What about you?

DONNY. *(Pause.)* I confess, so, to feeding him Frosties now and then, but only now and then, Padraic, and there does be nutrition in Frosties, and the fella seemed to like them.

PADRAIC. And that's all you confess? Well, straight to hell you'll be going, so, because I know well a hundred other crimes you've committed in your time.

DONNY. What other crimes?

PADRAIC. We don't have time to be making out a full list, but trampling on your mam all them times'll do for a start-off.

DAVEY. You *did* trample on your mam!

DONNY. Ten years ago, that was!

PADRAIC. There's no statute of limitations on mam trampling, Dad. Now shut up while I make me speech. *(Still pointing the guns at their heads, Padraic cocks them. Donny and Davey shiver tearfully. The clock on the wall is just reaching twelve ten.)* Ye have killed me cat and ye've ruined me life, for what I've got to live for now I do not know …

DAVEY. You could get another cat. *(Padraic hits Davey with the butt of his gun.)*

PADRAIC. I will plod on, I know, but no sense to it will there be with Thomas gone. No longer will his smiling eyes be there in the back of me head, egging me on, saying, "This is for me and for Ireland, Padraic. Remember that," as I'd lob a bomb at a pub, or

37

be shooting a builder. Me whole world's gone, and he'll never be coming back to me. *(Pause.)* What I want ye to remember, as the bullets come out through yere foreheads, is that this is all a fella can be expecting for being so bad to an innocent Irish cat. Goodbye to ye, now. *(Donny and Davey tense up.)* Goodbye, I said.

DAVEY. Goodbye …

DONNY. Goodbye, Padraic … *(Donny and Davey tense up again. Pause. There is a loud knock at the front door. Padraic uncocks his guns.)*

PADRAIC. *(Sighing.)* You could've told me you were expecting someone.

DONNY. I wasn't. *(Padraic goes to the door.)*

PADRAIC. Well, don't try anything or ye'll be getting it worse.

DAVEY. *(Whispered to Donny.)* Sure, how can we get it any worse, sure? *(Padraic opens the front door wide. Standing there are Christy, Joey and Brendan, smiling, their hands behind their backs. Padraic laughs, happy to see them.)*

CHRISTY. Howdo.

PADRAIC. Christy! What the feck are you fellas doing out this way? Come on in ahead for yourselves. I'm just in the middle of shooting me dad. *(He turns his back on them, goes back to the two kneeling men and points his guns at their heads, at the same time as the three men at the door dash in, take the guns out from behind their backs and point them right up against Padraic's head — one on the left side, one on the right and one from behind, in something of a triangle. Pause.)* What's all this about, now?

CHRISTY. Does the word "splinter group" mean anything to ya?

PADRAIC. "Splinter group"? Splinter group's two words.

CHRISTY. Mister Cocksure, uh-huh.

BRENDAN. Hah. He's not so cocksure now, is he, Christy?

CHRISTY. He's not.

JOEY. He *is.*

CHRISTY. Shush, now, Joey …

JOEY. Well, he *is.* He's still cocksure. Look at him …

CHRISTY. All *right,* Joey. For feck's *sake,* now. *(Pause.)* Throw your guns on the table there, Padraic, and easy. *(Padraic pauses a moment, then does so.)* Skank Toby was the last straw, Padraic. Messing around teasing your marijuana gobshites is fine. But when you drag one of the big-time boys into the equation, a fella without whom there'd be no financing for your ferry crossings and your chip-shop manoeuvres, and not only to cut the nose off him, all well and good, a bit of micro-surgery may do the trick later, but to then feed it to his cocker spaniel, a dog never did no one harm, and choked himself to death on it ...

PADRAIC. I don't like dogs, I don't.

DONNY. He was frightened be a corgi as a little fella.

CHRISTY. And made Skank Toby watch that dog choke, and sticking your finger in where his nose was then if he tried to help it, and when then you talk of splinter groups, and splinter groups of two fellas, which isn't a splinter group at all, it's just two fellas.

BRENDAN. In a mood.

CHRISTY. In a mood. No, boy. That's the time we've got to take a long hard look at ourselves and say "All this has got to end, now. Uh-huh. All this has got to end."

PADRAIC. You've always had it in for me, Christy. And for no reason at all.

CHRISTY. No reason, no. Other than you shooting me fecking eye out, ya bastard.

PADRAIC. I've apologised for that eye many's the day.

CHRISTY. Playing "murder in the dark" with a crossbow, like a schoolchild.

PADRAIC. You never let bygones be bygones, you. *(Christy cocks his gun. Joey and Brendan do likewise.)* Christy, now? You wouldn't be killing a fella in front of his dad, would ya?

BRENDAN. You're behind your dad.

PADRAIC. It's the *principle* I'm saying, ya thick, Brendan.

BRENDAN. Oh, the principle.

PADRAIC. Dad, you wouldn't want to see me killed in front of you, would ya? Wouldn't it be a trauma?

DONNY. I couldn't give a feck! Weren't you about to shoot me in the fecking head, sure?

PADRAIC. Ah, I was only tinkering with ya, Dad. Do you think I'd've done it?

DONNY. Aye!

DAVEY. Aye!

PADRAIC. Take me out on the road, Christy. No one ever comes down that lonely road. Not a struggle I'll give to ya. I knew this'd be coming some day. I just didn't think so soon, and from friends. Just walk me to a ditch. The burying will be all the easier for you. Only it'll give me a minute to be saying a prayer for me poor cat, died recently, the self-same road.

BRENDAN. *(Smiling.)* Your poor cat, is it?

PADRAIC. It is. Why?

CHRISTY. *(Raising a cautionary finger.)* Erm …

BRENDAN. *(Thinking quickly.)* Erm … We heard tell of your cat dying … and sad we were you were to have the two spots of bad news in the one week, your cat dying and your being shot through the brains yourself. That's awful hard luck.

PADRAIC. And I'll tell you this, boys. One of them spots of news does make me sadder than the other, but I'll bet in a hundred years you couldn't guess which.

JOEY. Your cat dying makes you sadder.

PADRAIC. Is right, Joey. You was always the sensitive one.

JOEY. Thank you, Padraic, I always tried.

CHRISTY. Tie his hands, Joe. We'll walk him the road for himself. For there's no terrible hard feelings in this execution. You was always a good soldier, Padraic. Just overenthusiastic. *(Joey ties Padraic's hands behind his back. Padraic looks around the room.)*

PADRAIC. Full of memories of Wee Thomas this house is. How asleep in me arms he'd fall, the armchair there. Aye, and purr and yawn. How he'd pooh in a corner when you were drunk and you'd forget to let him out, and he'd look embarrassed the next day then, as if it was his fault, the poor lamb. How in through the hole in the wall there he'd come, after a two-day bender chasing skirt the length of the island, and pulling your hair out for fear something had happened to him you'd be, and him prancing in then like "What was all the fuss about? I was off getting me end away." *(Pause.)* He won't be prancing in today.

DAVEY. *(Half laughing.)* Indeed he won't be.

PADRAIC. What d'you mean "Indeed he won't be?"

DAVEY. No, I'm just saying it does be awful hard to prance when you're buried in shite, your head knocked out your arse. *(His hands tied, Padraic tries to lunge out at Davey with his feet. The three gunmen restrain him and start dragging him to the door.)* Come on indeed, ya oul mad hole, ya!

40

PADRAIC. I'll fecking kill ya!

DAVEY. Kill me so, aye, and cut the rest of me hair off while you're at it, ya bully!

CHRISTY. Get him outside …

PADRAIC. Ya fecking cat killer, ya …

DAVEY. Eight years it took me to grow that hair!

PADRAIC. I'll be back to get ya! *(To Donny.)* And you too!

DAVEY. In your dreams you'll be back, ya lube.

PADRAIC. Not in me dreams at all. In ten minutes.

CHRISTY. You won't be back in ten minutes, Padraic. You'll be dead in ten minutes.

PADRAIC. We'll be seeing about that! I'd've gone easy till this feck chipped in!

CHRISTY. We have three guns to your head and you're bound be rope, sure.

PADRAIC. Something'll turn up!

JOEY. What does he mean, Christy? "Something'll turn up"?

CHRISTY. *(Exiting.)* He's just trying to make you nervous, Joey.

JOEY. *(Exiting.)* He's fecking succeeded, Christy.

BRENDAN. *(Exiting.)* Didn't I tell you he'd shit himself, Christy?

PADRAIC. *(Exiting.)* I'll be back again for you, long-hair boy!

DAVEY. Do! And bring your drippy cat with you! Ye can both take me on! Ye'd still lose!

PADRAIC. *(Distantly.)* Something'll turn up! I can feel it! *(Long silent pause. The gunmen and Padraic have gone. Donny and Davey are still tied, kneeling.)*

DAVEY. Has he always been that way, Donny?

DONNY. I think he may have gotten worse, now.

DAVEY. *(Pause.)* Are you sad, Donny?

DONNY. Sad, why?

DAVEY. Sad them fellas are to be shooting your son's head off him?

DONNY. *(Pause.)* Not really, if I think about it, now.

DAVEY. No. After your son tries to execute you, your opinions do change about him.

DONNY. You lose respect, d'you know?

DAVEY. *(Pause.)* They could've untied us. It wouldn't have killed them. *(Pause.)* Actually it *might've* killed them, come to think of it.

DONNY. It might've, aye. They had to concentrate at all times

41

with that mad feck.

DAVEY. Let them concentrate a minute more and that'll be the end of it. Your son will be dead and them fecks will be gone, and Inishmore can get back to normal then.

DONNY. Is right. It's incidents like this does put tourists off Ireland.

DAVEY. Aye. *(Pause.)* "He'll be back again for me." He isn't back yet, nor will he be back.

DONNY *(Pause.)* Did you hear a noise?

DAVEY. What kind of a noise?

DONNY. A clicking?

DAVEY. No.

DONNY. Oh.

DAVEY. Did you?

DONNY. No.

DAVEY. Oh.

DONNY. Good.

DAVEY. Aye. *(Pause, then the unmistakable sound of the rapid fire, from somewhere outside, of Mairead's air rifle ...)* Ar, not me fecking sister, now! (... *followed immediately by the hideous screaming of the three gunmen. Sound of gunfire being returned, as the screams continue, getting louder and louder as the screamers get nearer to the house, till suddenly Brendan smashes in through the window left and Joey and Christy burst in through the door. All three are bleeding profusely from their eyes, at which they clutch and tear, blinded, still screaming, crawling around the floor. Donny and Davey watch them in horror.)*

BRENDAN. I can't fecking see! I can't fecking see!

JOEY. She's had our fecking eyes out!

CHRISTY. Are ye blinded too?

BRENDAN. We fecking are!

CHRISTY. Was it a boy or was it a girl?

BRENDAN. It was a boy with lipstick.

JOEY. It was a girl with no boobs, sure.

BRENDAN. Oh, don't let me be killed by a girl, Sweet Jesus! I'll never live it down.

JOEY. Mam and Dad'll be terrible sad, eh, Brendan, the two of us killed the same day?

BRENDAN. Oh, they'll be choked, Joey. I *do* love you, y'know, Joe. I'm sorry if I never showed it ya.

JOEY. I love you too, Brendan!

CHRISTY. Ar, stop that shite! Get firing, now! *(All three gunmen begin shooting madly, Brendan through the left window, Christy through the right and Joey through the doorway.)* Are you two tied fellas still here?

DAVEY. Aye.

DONNY. Aye. No!!

DAVEY. No!! *(Donny quietly shoulder-knudges Davey in irritation for giving away their presence.)*

CHRISTY. Well call out the right direction for us to be shooting, so, or ye'll be getting it too. *(Just then, Padraic and Mairead appear in the doorway, hand in hand, quietly stepping around Joey's line of fire as they enter, Mairead carrying her air rifle, Padraic pulling the last of the ropes off his hands.)*

DONNY. *(To Christy.)* Erm, left a biteen ... *(The three gunmen, still firing out of the windows and door, aim towards the left. Padraic and Mairead seem to almost glide across the room, their eyes locked on each other. Padraic caresses her hair and cheek, impressed beyond words at her abilities with a gun.)* Erm, right a bit, now ...

BRENDAN. They must be zigzagging! Are they?

DONNY. They are.

BRENDAN. The fecks! *(The gunmen shoot towards the right. Padraic and Mairead step over to where the two handguns lie on the table and Padraic picks them up. They move up behind Brendan and, with Mairead caressing the muscles in his back and shoulders, Padraic puts both guns up to Brendan's head and fires, killing him instantly. With all the gunfire going on, the other two gunmen do not notice. Padraic and Mairead move slowly towards Joey, their eyes still locked in love.)*

CHRISTY. Are they getting nearer or are they getting away? *(Padraic shoots Joey in the head, again with the double-gun method at close quarters. Mairead gently toes Joey's dead body.)*

DONNY. They're getting nearer.

CHRISTY. How near?

DONNY. Awful near. *(Christy runs out of bullets. As he tries to reload he realises all the other gunfire has stopped too.)*

CHRISTY. Fellas? Why've you stopped shooting, fellas? Fellas? *(Pause. Christy's face drops as he realises Padraic is in the room. He tosses his gun away, sick.)* Not in me head, Padraic, please. For me mother's sake, now ... *(Padraic double-shoots Christy in the chest. Christy slumps back on to the floor, dying, but not actually dead. Padraic and Mairead move up to each other and kiss, as Donny and Davey look on, still kneeling there, bound and trembling.)*

DONNY. That was some gutsy shooting, Padraic!

DAVEY. What's he kissing me fecking sister for? *(Padraic and Mairead slowly turn and look at the two. Padraic cocks his guns. The two tremble.)*

PADRAIC. This fella's your brother, is he?

MAIREAD. He has a better hairstyle since last I saw him, but aye, he is.

PADRAIC. Oh. I was all set to blow his head off now, along with the feck beside him, but if he's family I won't. I'll have some respect. I'll kill me dad on his own. *(Mairead gently takes one of the guns from Padraic, sidles up behind her brother and puts the gun to his head, speaking as she goes.)*

MAIREAD. If I'm to be travelling back up North with you, I suppose I'll have to be getting used to proper guns some time.

PADRAIC. And there's no time like the present.

MAIREAD. None at all. *(They smile at each other. Padraic puts his gun to his dad's head, Mairead to Davey's.)*

DONNY. No, now ...

DAVEY. Ar, come on, now ...

DONNY. You're only tinkering with us again, aren't ye?

PADRAIC. On a count of three?

MAIREAD. On a count of three, aye. Like in films.

DAVEY. Ar, Jesus, Mairead, Jesus...!

PADRAIC. One...!

DONNY. Goodbye now, Davey ...

DAVEY. Goodbye now, Donny ...

PADRAIC. Two...!

DONNY. Unfair, this is!

DAVEY. Aren't they beggars?

PADRAIC. Three...!

CHRISTY. *(Interrupting.)* I'm sorry for killing your cat, Padraic.

I am, now.

PADRAIC. *(Pause.)* What was that, Christy?

CHRISTY. I said I'm sorry for killing your cat on you. The worst part of all this was that cat braining, but you had to be knocked off your guard some way, and you'll admit how well it worked, now. Ar, boy. Just making me peace with God, I am, in the seconds before I slip away, now.

PADRAIC. Your peace, is it?

CHRISTY. It is.

PADRAIC. Uh-huh. I'll give you some fecking peace, boy … *(Padraic and Mairead take their guns away from the kneelers' heads, Padraic chucks his on the table, goes over to Christy and starts dragging him by the neck into the adjoining room forward right, perhaps so that he's half out of sight. To Mairead:)* Bring a knife, a cheese grate, a razor, an iron and anything to gag the screaming, Mairead.

MAIREAD. Check, Lieutenant. *(Mairead puts her gun on the table and darts about, grabbing the objects just listed. Christy begins screaming hideously as Padraic tortures him, blood splattering.)*

DONNY. It's an ill wind that doesn't blow some fecker good!

DAVEY. Isn't it, though? *(Blackout.)*

45

SCENE NINE

Donny's house, night. As the scene begins the blood-soaked living room is strewn with the body parts of Brendan and Joey, which Donny and Davey, blood-soaked also, hack away at to sizeable chunks. Padraic's two guns are lying on the table. In the adjacent bare room, Padraic is sitting on Christy's corpse, stroking Wee Thomas's headless, dirt-soiled body. Through Christy's mouth, with the pointed end sticking out of the back of his neck, has been shoved the cross with "Wee Thomas" on it. Padraic has a sad, faraway look about him. He cannot hear the quiet conversation Donny and Davey are having.

DONNY. Won't your man be upset, your Mairead joining the paramilitaries, Davey?

DAVEY. She knew it was to be coming some day. I think she'll have resigned herself to it, though I think she'd have preferred it to be the IRA if anybody. Y'know, they're more established.

DONNY. They are. And they do travel further afield than the INLA.

DAVEY. The IRA do get a good bit of travelling done, aye.

DONNY. They do. They go to Belgium sometimes.

DAVEY. You never see the INLA going to Belgium.

DONNY. You're lucky if they leave the Falls.

DAVEY. You never see the INLA shooting Australians.

DONNY. Still, I suppose it isn't the travel that attracts people to the IRA.

DAVEY. No. It's the principle of the thing. I'll tell ya, I'd shit meself having to shoot fellas, but Mairead seems to have no qualms.

DONNY. I'll say this about Mairead. She's fecking accurate. Knock your eye out from a mile.

DAVEY. I always knew that cow practising would pay off some day.

46

DONNY. Padraic has an entirely different style.

DAVEY. Padraic goes all the way up to ya.

DONNY. Padraic goes all the way up to ya, and then uses two guns from only an inch away.

DAVEY. Sure, there's no skill in that.

DONNY. I think the two guns is overdoing it. From that range, like.

DAVEY. It's just showing off, really.

DONNY. Mairead sees more of the sport. *(Pause.)* Is he still sitting on the fella and stroking the dead cat?

DAVEY. *(Craning his neck.)* He is. Morbid, that was, digging up his dead cat. After all the trouble we went to burying it, and without a word of thanks.

DONNY. I suppose it does help the mourning process.

DAVEY. *(Pause.)* Digging up the corpse? *(Donny shrugs. Mairead has entered through the front door, wearing a pretty dress and carrying a rucksack and air rifle.)*

MAIREAD. Less gabbing and more chopping would be more in ye's two's line.

DONNY. I don't see you or your boyfriend giving us a hand …

DAVEY. What the hell's that you're wearing?

MAIREAD. A dress! I *do* have them!

DAVEY. Hrmm …

MAIREAD. Why should we be giving ye a hand?

DONNY. It's yere mess, sure.

MAIREAD. Well, it's your house. And you don't be getting officers doing this sort of dirty work, anyways.

DAVEY. Oh, you're an officer now, are ya?

MAIREAD. I'm a second-lieutenant. Just awarded be Padraic. Padraic's just awarded himself a full-blown lieutenantship, and he deserves it.

DONNY. Ye're all going up in the world.

MAIREAD. Be knocking them teeth out them mouths, now. It does hamper the identification process.

DONNY. She's awful on the ball.

MAIREAD. I am.

DAVEY. What did Mam say to you when you left?

MAIREAD. She said good luck and try not to go blowing up kids.

DAVEY. And what did you say?

47

MAIREAD. I said I'd try but I'd be making no promises.

DAVEY. And what did she say?

MAIREAD. She said so long as you try is the main thing.

DAVEY. I suppose it is.

MAIREAD. Oh, it is, but I can't be bandying about pleasantries with the likes of ye. Be getting on with your work, now. Them corpses won't be chopping themselves up, or d'ye think they will? *(Mairead passes through to Padraic.)*

DAVEY. She loves pegging orders, that one.

DONNY. I can see. *(Donny and Davey continue with their hacking and bludgeoning. Mairead sits down beside Padraic on Christy's bloody corpse.)*

MAIREAD. Howdo.

PADRAIC. Howdo. *(Pause.)* There's no head at all on Wee Thomas now.

MAIREAD. No. Does it make you think twice about the INLA, so, that they let fellas like Christy in, would do that to a cat?

PADRAIC. Sure, you do get bad apples in every organisation. *(Pause.)* Are them wet fellas still chopping?

MAIREAD. Aye.

PADRAIC. Are they making a decent job of it?

MAIREAD. Middling.

PADRAIC. They've had no practice, sure, God bless them. *(Pause.)* What the hell's that you're wearing?

MAIREAD. Isn't a girl allowed to wear dresses now and again?

PADRAIC. Just that it comes as a shock is all.

MAIREAD. Would you say I looked pretty in it, or just fair, now? *(Padraic kisses her at length, the cat awkward in one hand. They break after a few seconds.)*

PADRAIC. When you get up close to you, you don't really look like a boy at all.

MAIREAD. Thank you.

PADRAIC. Just except for your hair.

MAIREAD. From you that's some kind of compliment, I suppose?

PADRAIC. Would you let your hair be growing out a tadeen, Mairead? Just to about here, now. Like Evie off *The House of Elliot?*

MAIREAD. Would you like me to?

PADRAIC. Aye.

MAIREAD. Well, me hair's staying the way it is and feck Evie off *The House of Elliot.*

PADRAIC. Ah, Mairead ...

MAIREAD. Could Evie blind three fellas from sixty yards?

PADRAIC. No. But she probably wouldn't want to.

MAIREAD. Just be content with what you've fecking got, so.

PADRAIC. You're a tough oul get.

MAIREAD. And fecking proud of it.

PADRAIC. Kiss me again.

MAIREAD. I will.

PADRAIC. *(They kiss again. Pause.)* Will we leave the INLA altogether and be starting our own splinter group, just me and you?

MAIREAD. Would you like to?

PADRAIC. I would.

MAIREAD. We will so. What will we call ourselves?

PADRAIC. I was thinking "Wee Thomas's Army," unless you have an objection, now.

MAIREAD. Sure, that sounds like a great name. "Wee Thomas's Army." Aye. What'll be our first plan of action?

PADRAIC. Our first plan of action will be to find a fella I owe a torturing to. I had him in me clutches yesterday, but the cat distractions made me go easy on the feck, I hardly touched him, and he spun me a yarn about ringworm proved completely untrue too. "Wrapping pellets up in cheese." I bet he doesn't even have a cat.

MAIREAD. He sounds like a valid target anyways.

PADRAIC. He's the validest of targets.

MAIREAD. We should make a list of valid targets. From one to twenty. Like *Top of the Pops.*

PADRAIC. I used to have a list of valid targets but I lost it on a bus. Who would be top of your list?

MAIREAD. People who brain cats for no reason.

PADRAIC. Is a good target. Although ... *(Pause.)* Can I tell you this, Mairead? I did brain a cat this morning, but I did have a reason.

MAIREAD. What was the reason?

PADRAIC. It seemed terrible unhygienic. Half covered in black muck.

MAIREAD. Fair go, so. I don't like unhygienic cats. Braining nice clean cats, I'm saying. My cat I wanted to say goodbye to him, now

49

I won't be seeing him for a while. Me best friend in the world he is, but he wasn't about. He must be off gallivanting.

PADRAIC. My cat won't be off gallivanting no more, and he liked a good gallivant.

MAIREAD. Ar, Padraic …

PADRAIC. Ah, Mairead. Y'know, all I ever wanted was an Ireland free. Free for kids to run and play. Free for fellas and lasses to dance and sing. Free for cats to roam about without being clanked in the brains with a handgun. Was that too much to ask, now? Was it?

MAIREAD. It seems it was, Padraic. It seems it was. Will we be bringing Wee Thomas with us or will we be burying him here?

PADRAIC. We'll bring him with us. I have a window box at home he can go in, so he'll be near his friends.

MAIREAD. *(Standing.)* Would you want to bring his crucifix, so?

PADRAIC. *(Standing.)* No. That crucifix is too big for my window box. It'd break me chrysanthemums. *(Hand in hand, they enter the living room.)* How is the work going, ye's two?

DONNY. We're almost there, Padraic. Almost there.

PADRAIC. You're not almost there at all, sure. The fingerprints you haven't burnt off and the teeth you haven't bludgeoned out. And One-eyed Christy you haven't even started on. "Ye're almost there." You won't be almost there for a week, sure.

DAVEY. Why we should be doing this work at all I don't see. It wasn't us murdered them. If it was us murdered them I'd say "fair go," but no.

PADRAIC. Are you grumbling again, you?

DAVEY. *(Mumbling.)* I fecking am.

PADRAIC. Eh?

DAVEY. No, I'm not grumbling.

PADRAIC. I'd've been kicking your balls out your brains long since, you, ya feck, only it's sure I am you'll be being me brother-in-law some day, and that'd be a bad show that'd be, kicking your brother-in-law's balls out his brains. *(Mairead gazes up at Padraic lovingly.)*

MAIREAD. Is it marriage you're proposing to me so, Padraic Osbourne?

PADRAIC. It is. After a biteen of a while I'm saying, now. When our work is done.

MAIREAD. When Ireland is free!

PADRAIC. Indeed when Ireland is free! *(They kiss at length.)*

DONNY. That'll be a long fecking engagement!

DAVEY. Fecking a hundred they'll be, and still waiting.

DONNY. Won't that make you and me related so, when them two marry?

DAVEY. *(With disdain.)* It fecking will too.

DONNY. What matter?

DAVEY. Do you think I want to be related to mad gunmen and mam tramplers?

DONNY. Do you think I want to be related to gay hippies and cat polishers?

DAVEY. *(Quietly, in awful realisation.)* Oh, feck, now! All about that fecking cat I forgot! *(Davey goes over to the bloody cat basket on the table stage left, checks inside for the cat but finds it empty, puts the basket aside, looks around a little more, shoving a head or an arm aside, then finds Sir Roger's collar and name tag on the cabinet stage left. He is just about to toss it out through the broken window when Padraic and Mairead separate.)*

PADRAIC. Look at you in that pretty dress. Oh, God, now! Half-covered it in blood we have.

MAIREAD. Ah, what matter? Red goes well with it.

PADRAIC. You can't go walking the streets of Ulster dripping blood, now.

MAIREAD. Sure, who would notice, Padraic?

PADRAIC. Tourists would notice. Be changing it or washing it off, now.

MAIREAD. I'll give it a wee rinse for meself, so. *(Davey tosses the collar out through the window.)* What are you up to?

DAVEY. Nothing at all.

MAIREAD. Be desecting them fecks, you.

DAVEY. I was just waving me arms.

MAIREAD. Uh-huh. And you say Padraic's mad? *(She moves towards bathroom left.)* Can you bear to be away from me five minutes, me love?

PADRAIC. I can't. Be hurrying.

MAIREAD. I will. *(Mairead blows him a kiss and exits into bathroom.)*

51

PADRAIC. *(Calling out.)* Oh, and be minding that oul grubby cat on the floor there I did blow the guts out of. *(Davey's mouth drops slightly and he stares off towards the bathroom. To Davey:)* So you be saying I'm mad, do ya?

DAVEY. *(Absently.)* I do.

PADRAIC. Eh?

DAVEY. Eh?

PADRAIC. I'm saying you be saying I'm mad, do ya?

DAVEY. *(Absently.)* I do.

PADRAIC. Eh?!

DAVEY. Eh? *(Davey looks across at Padraic for the first time, unaware of any discourtesy.)*

PADRAIC. You're a funny little fella. Be getting back to work, now. Do you think them corpses'll be chopping themselves up?

DONNY. They won't be, Padraic. Davey, what's the matter with you? Come back down here and start hammering some teeth.

DAVEY. *(Absently.)* I'll be hammering, aye. *(He kneels back down beside Donny and starts absent-mindedly hammering the teeth out of one of the heads, his eyes on the bathroom all the while.)* Worse and worse and worse this story gets.

DONNY. What are you saying, Davey?

DAVEY. Worse and fecking worse.

PADRAIC. That boy's near simple.

DONNY. He's an odd little gasur. He seems to have no proper sense. *(Pause. Sawing.)* Boy, spines are awful hard sawing, I'll tell ya.

PADRAIC. Aren't they, though? Be aiming for the vertebree is easiest.

DONNY. The vertebree, I was thinking. *(Mairead appears blank-eyed in the doorway of the bathroom, clutching the body of the bloody and black Sir Roger to her chest. Davey has seen her, the other two haven't.)* Have I congratulated you on your engagement yet, son?

PADRAIC. You haven't.

DONNY. *(Getting up.)* Congratulations on your engagement, son.

PADRAIC. Thanks, Dad. *(Donny shakes Padraic's hand. Mairead enters the room and Padraic notices her for the first time.)* Look at you. We have a matching pair. One fecked cat each. Who says we have nothing in common but shooting fellas? No, I shouldn't be joking like that. Not about poor Wee Thomas, now.

MAIREAD. Not about Sir Roger neither, no.

PADRAIC. Sir Roger who? Sir Roger Casement?

MAIREAD. Aye.

PADRAIC. What has that oul poof got to do with dead cats, Mairead? *(Mairead gently hands her cat down to Davey, smiles slightly at him and brushes a bloody hand through his short hair. She turns back to Padraic, whose back is to the table, the two handguns behind him. He caresses her cheek gently, as she quietly begins singing "The Dying Rebel.")*

MAIREAD. *(Singing.)* "The night was dark and the fight was ended ... " *(Padraic joins in.)*

BOTH. "The moon shone down O'Connell Street ... "

MAIREAD. Kiss me, Padraic. *(Padraic kisses her at length and, as he does so, Mairead reaches down behind him, picks one gun up in each hand, slowly raises them and points them one on each side of Padraic's head. Padraic is unaware of this. Donny looks on in horror. The kiss is finished.)*

PADRAIC. What's the next line now, Mairead? *(Singing.)* "The moon shone down O'Connell Street ..."

MAIREAD. There was nothing unhygienic about my fecking cat.

PADRAIC. *(Pause.)* No, it's something to do with brave men perishing, I think.

MAIREAD. Aye. *(She shoots Padraic in the head with both guns. Padraic falls back on the table behind him, dead, his cat still clutched in his arms, his mouth wide open. Mairead looks at the guns in her hands a while, as she quietly continues with the song. Singing.)* "I stood alone where brave men perished. Those men have gone, their God to meet." *(She places the barrels of both guns in Padraic's mouth, leaves them there and gently takes her cat back off Davey.)* Be chopping up that feck too, now, the two of ye.

DONNY. Sure, you can't be asking me to go chopping up me own son, now!

DAVEY. Well, *I'm* not doing all the work! I'll tell you that!

MAIREAD. One of ye's chop up Padraic, the other be chopping the fella there with the cross in his gob. And don't be countermanding me orders, cos it's a fecking lieutenant ye're talking to now.

DAVEY. *(To Donny.)* That sounds fairer, splitting the workload.

DONNY. I suppose. *(Mairead collects up her rucksack and air rifle.)*

53

DAVEY. Is it still off to the INLA you're going, Mairead?

DONNY. *(Waving a hand at the carnage.)* Sure, there's no fecker left in the INLA now!

MAIREAD. No, David. I think I'll be staying around here for a biteen. I thought shooting fellas would be fun, but it's not. It's dull.

DAVEY. It gets boring easy.

MAIREAD. Aye.

DONNY. Aye. Stick to cows. *(Mairead gives Donny an evil look. Scared.)* I'm upset over the death of me son, Mairead.

MAIREAD. *(Pause.)* I'm off home with Sir Roger. Be getting on with your chopping you two.

DAVEY. Aye.

DONNY. Aye. *(They linger.)*

MAIREAD. *(Angrily.)* Be getting on, I'm saying! That's an order! *(Donny and Davey tut, kneel down and start hacking up the body parts again.)* And it's an investigation tomorrow I'll be launching, when I've had a chance to think, about how Sir Roger came to end up in this house in the first place, and half black with it. *(Donny and Davey wince, their shoulders slumping, as they continue with their work. Singing.)* "My only son was shot in Dublin, fighting for his country bold. He fought for Ireland and Ireland only. The harp and shamrock, green, white and gold." *(Mairead exits. After they're sure she's gone, Donny and Davey stop work, still kneeling there, and hold their heads in their hands, groaning.)*

DAVEY. Oh, will it never end? Will it never fecking end?

DONNY. It fecking won't, d'you know! *(Slight pause. A black cat scrambles through the hole high in the wall stage left and stands or walks along the shelf there. Donny and Davey look at each other, then slowly turn and look at the cat.)*

DAVEY. What the hell fecking cat is that, now? *(Donny gets up and goes over to it.)*

DONNY. *(Sickened.)* Fecking Wee fecking Thomas this fecking is!

DAVEY. No!

DONNY. Aye!

DAVEY. How?

DONNY. Off fecking gallivanting he must've been these two fecking days!

DAVEY. Off chasing fecking skirt!

DONNY. Aye! *(Davey gets up and looks at the cat in Padraic's arms on the table.)*

DAVEY. So who the feck is this fecking cat?

DONNY. Some fecking stray that must've been, only looked like Wee Thomas.

DAVEY. So all this terror has been for absolutely nothing?

DONNY. It has!

DAVEY. All because that fecker was after his hole? Four dead fellas, two dead cats ... me hairstyle ruined! Have I missed anything?

DONNY. Your sister broken-hearted.

DAVEY. Me sister broken-hearted.

DONNY. All me shoe polish gone.

DAVEY. That cat deserves shooting!

DONNY. He does, d'you know?

DAVEY. *(Pause. Thinking about it.)* He does, d'you know? *(Davey slowly turns and looks at the guns in Padraic's mouth. He waves a thumb at them. The two look at each other a moment, then go over and each pull a gun out of Padraic. Donny picks the cat up off the shelf, or wherever he's got to, and places him on a clear spot, on the table beside Padraic. They both cock their guns and slowly raise them till they're pointed at the cat.)*

DONNY. But Davey...?

DAVEY. What? *(They lower their guns.)*

DONNY. Hasn't there been enough killing done in this house for one day?

DAVEY. *(Pause.)* No.

DONNY. One more won't fecking hurt! *(They both aim their guns at the cat's head again, arms taut.)* On a count of three, now.

DAVEY. Aye.

BOTH. *(Pause.)* One ... *(Pause.)* Two ... *(Pause.)* Three! *(A long, long pause, arms taut, teeth gritted, not breathing. But neither of them can bring himself to do it.)*

DONNY. *(Teeth gritted.)* Will we leave the poor beggar alone, Davey?

DAVEY. *(Teeth gritted.)* Will we, Donny?

DONNY. We will!

DAVEY. We will! *(The two breathe a sigh of relief, hearts pounding, slam the guns down on the table and stroke and pet the cat, trying to*

recover their breath.) There there, Wee Thomas. There there ...
(Donny pours Wee Thomas some Frosties.)
DONNY. There there, now, baby. Sure, you're home now. You're home now.
DAVEY. Home sweet home.
DONNY. Home sweet home is right! *(Fade to black as the cat eats the Frosties.)* Didn't I tell you he likes Frosties, Davey? *(If, however, the cat doesn't eat the Frosties, the above line should be substituted for:)*
DAVEY. He doesn't like Frosties at all, Donny. *(Blackout.)*

End of Play

PROPERTY LIST

Dead black cat
Live black cat
Ginger cat
Dead ginger cat
Telephone
Cat's collar and name tag
3 guns
Wooden cross
Cat basket
Dismembered corpses
Pink bicycle (DAVEY)
Razor (PADRAIC, MAIREAD)
2 handguns (PADRAIC)
Cell phone (PADRAIC)
Bicycle pump (DAVEY)
Air rifle (MAIREAD)
Bottle of poteen (DONNY)
Black shoe polish (DAVEY)
Can of beans (CHRISTY)
Pieces of rope (PADRAIC, JOEY)
Bowie knife (PADRAIC)
Cheese grater (MAIREAD)
Iron (MAIREAD)
Gag (MAIREAD)
Rucksack (MAIREAD)
Box of Frosties and bowl (DONNY)

SOUND EFFECTS

Cell phone ringing
Gunshots
Air rifle shots

NEW PLAYS

★ **YELLOW FACE by David Henry Hwang.** Asian-American playwright DHH leads a protest against the casting of Jonathan Pryce as the Eurasian pimp in the original Broadway production of *Miss Saigon,* condemning the practice as "yellowface." The lines between truth and fiction blur with hilarious and moving results in this unreliable memoir. "A pungent play of ideas with a big heart." *—Variety.* "Fabulously inventive." *—The New Yorker.* [5M, 2W] ISBN: 978-0-8222-2301-6

★ **33 VARIATIONS by Moisés Kaufmann.** A mother coming to terms with her daughter. A composer coming to terms with his genius. And, even though they're separated by 200 years, these two people share an obsession that might, even just for a moment, make time stand still. "A compellingly original and thoroughly watchable play for today." *—Talkin' Broadway.* [4M, 4W] ISBN: 978-0-8222-2392-4

★ **BOOM by Peter Sinn Nachtrieb.** A grad student's online personal ad lures a mysterious journalism student to his subterranean research lab. But when a major catastrophic event strikes the planet, their date takes on evolutionary significance and the fate of humanity hangs in the balance. "Darkly funny dialogue." *—NY Times.* "Literate, coarse, thoughtful, sweet, scabrously inappropriate." *—Washington City Paper.* [1M, 2W] ISBN: 978-0-8222-2370-2

★ **LOVE, LOSS AND WHAT I WORE by Nora Ephron and Delia Ephron, based on the book by Ilene Beckerman.** A play of monologues and ensemble pieces about women, clothes and memory covering all the important subjects—mothers, prom dresses, mothers, buying bras, mothers, hating purses and why we only wear black. "Funny, compelling." *—NY Times.* "So funny and so powerful." *—WowOwow.com.* [5W] ISBN: 978-0-8222-2355-9

★ **CIRCLE MIRROR TRANSFORMATION by Annie Baker.** When four lost New Englanders enrolled in Marty's community center drama class experiment with harmless games, hearts are quietly torn apart, and tiny wars of epic proportions are waged and won. "Absorbing, unblinking and sharply funny." *—NY Times.* [2M, 3W] ISBN: 978-0-8222-2445-7

★ **BROKE-OLOGY by Nathan Louis Jackson.** The King family has weathered the hardships of life and survived with their love for each other intact. But when two brothers are called home to take care of their father, they find themselves strangely at odds. "Engaging dialogue." *—TheaterMania.com.* "Assured, bighearted." *—Time Out.* [3M, 1W] ISBN: 978-0-8222-2428-0

DRAMATISTS PLAY SERVICE, INC.
440 Park Avenue South, New York, NY 10016 212-683-8960 Fax 212-213-1539
postmaster@dramatists.com www.dramatists.com

NEW PLAYS

★ **A CIVIL WAR CHRISTMAS: AN AMERICAN MUSICAL CELEBRA-TION by Paula Vogel, music by Daryl Waters.** It's 1864, and Washington, D.C. is settling down to the coldest Christmas Eve in years. Intertwining many lives, this musical shows us that the gladness of one's heart is the best gift of all. "Boldly inventive theater, warm and affecting." –*Talkin' Broadway.* "Crisp strokes of dialogue." –*NY Times.* [12M, 5W] ISBN: 978-0-8222-2361-0

★ **SPEECH & DEBATE by Stephen Karam.** Three teenage misfits in Salem, Oregon discover they are linked by a sex scandal that's rocked their town. "Savvy comedy." –*Variety.* "Hilarious, cliché-free, and immensely entertaining." –*NY Times.* "A strong, rangy play." –*NY Newsday.* [2M, 2W] ISBN: 978-0-8222-2286-6

★ **DIVIDING THE ESTATE by Horton Foote.** Matriarch Stella Gordon is determined not to divide her 100-year-old Texas estate, despite her family's declining wealth and the looming financial crisis. But her three children have another plan. "Goes for laughs and succeeds." –*NY Daily News.* "The theatrical equivalent of a page-turner." –*Bloomberg.com.* [4M, 9W] ISBN: 978-0-8222-2398-6

★ **WHY TORTURE IS WRONG, AND THE PEOPLE WHO LOVE THEM by Christopher Durang.** Christopher Durang turns political humor upside down with this raucous and provocative satire about America's growing homeland "insecurity." "A smashing new play." –*NY Observer.* "You may laugh yourself silly." –*Bloomberg News.* [4M, 3W] ISBN: 978-0-8222-2401-3

★ **FIFTY WORDS by Michael Weller.** While their nine-year-old son is away for the night on his first sleepover, Adam and Jan have an evening alone together, beginning a suspenseful nightlong roller-coaster ride of revelation, rancor, passion and humor. "Mr. Weller is a bold and productive dramatist." –*NY Times.* [1M, 1W] ISBN: 978-0-8222-2348-1

★ **BECKY'S NEW CAR by Steven Dietz.** Becky Foster is caught in middle age, middle management and in a middling marriage—with no prospects for change on the horizon. Then one night a socially inept and grief-struck millionaire stumbles into the car dealership where Becky works. "Gently and consistently funny." –*Variety.* "Perfect blend of hilarious comedy and substantial weight." –*Broadway Hour.* [4M, 3W] ISBN: 978-0-8222-2393-1

DRAMATISTS PLAY SERVICE, INC.
440 Park Avenue South, New York, NY 10016 212-683-8960 Fax 212-213-1539
postmaster@dramatists.com www.dramatists.com

NEW PLAYS

★ **AT HOME AT THE ZOO by Edward Albee.** Edward Albee delves deeper into his play THE ZOO STORY by adding a first act, HOMELIFE, which precedes Peter's fateful meeting with Jerry on a park bench in Central Park. "An essential and heartening experience." –*NY Times.* "Darkly comic and thrilling." –*Time Out.* "Genuinely fascinating." –*Journal News.* [2M, 1W] ISBN: 978-0-8222-2317-7

★ **PASSING STRANGE book and lyrics by Stew, music by Stew and Heidi Rodewald, created in collaboration with Annie Dorsen.** A daring musical about a young bohemian that takes you from black middle-class America to Amsterdam, Berlin and beyond on a journey towards personal and artistic authenticity. "Fresh, exuberant, bracingly inventive, bitingly funny, and full of heart." –*NY Times.* "The freshest musical in town!" –*Wall Street Journal.* "Excellent songs and a vulnerable heart." –*Variety.* [4M, 3W] ISBN: 978-0-8222-2400-6

★ **REASONS TO BE PRETTY by Neil LaBute.** Greg really, truly adores his girlfriend, Steph. Unfortunately, he also thinks she has a few physical imperfections, and when he mentions them, all hell breaks loose. "Tight, tense and emotionally true." –*Time Magazine.* "Lively and compulsively watchable." –*The Record.* [2M, 2W] ISBN: 978-0-8222-2394-8

★ **OPUS by Michael Hollinger.** With only a few days to rehearse a grueling Beethoven masterpiece, a world-class string quartet struggles to prepare their highest-profile performance ever—a televised ceremony at the White House. "Intimate, intense and profoundly moving." –*Time Out.* "Worthy of scores of bravissimos." –*BroadwayWorld.com.* [4M, 1W] ISBN: 978-0-8222-2363-4

★ **BECKY SHAW by Gina Gionfriddo.** When an evening calculated to bring happiness takes a dark turn, crisis and comedy ensue in this wickedly funny play that asks what we owe the people we love and the strangers who land on our doorstep. "As engrossing as it is ferociously funny." –*NY Times.* "Gionfriddo is some kind of genius." –*Variety.* [2M, 3W] ISBN: 978-0-8222-2402-0

★ **KICKING A DEAD HORSE by Sam Shepard.** Hobart Struther's horse has just dropped dead. In an eighty-minute monologue, he discusses what path brought him here in the first place, the fate of his marriage, his career, politics and eventually the nature of the universe. "Deeply instinctual and intuitive." –*NY Times.* "The brilliance is in the infinite reverberations Shepard extracts from his simple metaphor." –*TheaterMania.* [1M, 1W] ISBN: 978-0-8222-2336-8

DRAMATISTS PLAY SERVICE, INC.
440 Park Avenue South, New York, NY 10016 212-683-8960 Fax 212-213-1539
postmaster@dramatists.com www.dramatists.com

NEW PLAYS

★ **AUGUST: OSAGE COUNTY by Tracy Letts.** WINNER OF THE 2008 PULITZER PRIZE AND TONY AWARD. When the large Weston family reunites after Dad disappears, their Oklahoma homestead explodes in a maelstrom of repressed truths and unsettling secrets. "Fiercely funny and bitingly sad." –*NY Times.* "Ferociously entertaining." –*Variety.* "A hugely ambitious, highly combustible saga." –*NY Daily News.* [6M, 7W] ISBN: 978-0-8222-2300-9

★ **RUINED by Lynn Nottage.** WINNER OF THE 2009 PULITZER PRIZE. Set in a small mining town in Democratic Republic of Congo, RUINED is a haunting, probing work about the resilience of the human spirit during times of war. "A full-immersion drama of shocking complexity and moral ambiguity." –*Variety.* "Sincere, passionate, courageous." –*Chicago Tribune.* [8M, 4W] ISBN: 978-0-8222-2390-0

★ **GOD OF CARNAGE by Yasmina Reza, translated by Christopher Hampton.** WINNER OF THE 2009 TONY AWARD. A playground altercation between boys brings together their Brooklyn parents, leaving the couples in tatters as the rum flows and tensions explode. "Satisfyingly primitive entertainment." –*NY Times.* "Elegant, acerbic, entertainingly fueled on pure bile." –*Variety.* [2M, 2W] ISBN: 978-0-8222-2399-3

★ **THE SEAFARER by Conor McPherson.** Sharky has returned to Dublin to look after his irascible, aging brother. Old drinking buddies Ivan and Nicky are holed up at the house too, hoping to play some cards. But with the arrival of a stranger from the distant past, the stakes are raised ever higher. "Dark and enthralling Christmas fable." –*NY Times.* "A timeless classic." –*Hollywood Reporter.* [5M] ISBN: 978-0-8222-2284-2

★ **THE NEW CENTURY by Paul Rudnick.** When the playwright is Paul Rudnick, expectations are geared for a play both hilarious and smart, and this provocative and outrageous comedy is no exception. "The one-liners fly like rockets." –*NY Times.* "The funniest playwright around." –*Journal News.* [2M, 3W] ISBN: 978-0-8222-2315-3

★ **SHIPWRECKED! AN ENTERTAINMENT—THE AMAZING ADVENTURES OF LOUIS DE ROUGEMONT (AS TOLD BY HIMSELF) by Donald Margulies.** The amazing story of bravery, survival and celebrity that left nineteenth-century England spellbound. Dare to be whisked away. "A deft, literate narrative." –*LA Times.* "Springs to life like a theatrical pop-up book." –*NY Times.* [2M, 1W] ISBN: 978-0-8222-2341-2

DRAMATISTS PLAY SERVICE, INC.
440 Park Avenue South, New York, NY 10016 212-683-8960 Fax 212-213-1539
postmaster@dramatists.com www.dramatists.com